Game Development with Unity: Create Your First 2D Game from Scratch

A Complete Guide to Game Design and Development with Unity

MIGUEL FARMER

RAFAEL SANDERS

Table of Content

TABLE OF CONTENTS

INTRODUCTION

Game Development with Unity: Create Your First 2D Game from Scratch

Welcome to *Game Development with Unity: Create Your First 2D Game from Scratch.* Whether you're an aspiring game developer or a seasoned professional looking to expand your skill set, this book is designed to guide you through every stage of building a 2D game using Unity, one of the most powerful and accessible game engines available today.

The Power of Unity for Game Development

Unity has become the go-to engine for both beginner and professional game developers. It offers an intuitive interface, robust tools, and a massive supportive community. From indie developers to AAA studios, Unity provides everything you need to bring your game ideas to life. Its versatility allows you to create 2D games, 3D experiences, virtual reality simulations, and much more, all within one platform.

Why 2D? Even though Unity is known for its capabilities in 3D game development, creating 2D games remains an important and exciting part of the game development landscape. 2D games often focus on pure gameplay mechanics, storytelling, and art direction. They're simpler to develop but still offer great depth, creativity, and complexity. Building a 2D game in Unity provides an excellent starting point for understanding the fundamentals of game development while offering a highly satisfying and tangible project to work on.

The Structure of This Book

This book is structured to take you through the entire game development process, starting from the very basics and moving toward more advanced topics, making it ideal for both beginners and those with some game development experience. It is broken down into 27 chapters, each focusing on a specific aspect of creating your 2D game, from setting up your first Unity project to polishing your final game for release.

Throughout the chapters, you'll encounter practical, real-world examples. These examples will help you understand how to apply what you learn directly to your own game projects. We're not interested in overcomplicated theory or unnecessary jargon. Instead, we'll focus on clear, actionable steps and tips that you can use right away to improve your development skills.

Who This Book Is For

If you've never touched a game engine before, this book is for you. We'll start from the very basics, helping you understand how Unity works and how to use its many features. You don't need prior programming experience. As long as you have a basic understanding of computers and are eager to learn, you'll be able to dive in and start making your first game.

However, if you're an experienced developer or have worked with other game engines before, don't worry—this book is designed to offer you more than just an introduction. You'll encounter advanced scripting techniques, optimization tips, and real-world examples to help you fine-tune your skills and take your projects to the next level.

What You'll Learn

- **Unity Interface and Tools**: You'll become familiar with the Unity interface and how to use its 2D tools effectively. We'll guide you through setting up your first 2D project, importing assets, and organizing your workflow for efficiency.

- **Scripting and Game Mechanics**: You'll learn how to script in C# to control player movement, interactions, and game logic. Whether you're creating a simple platformer or an adventure game, the principles you'll learn here apply to all genres of 2D games.
- **Physics and Animation**: Learn how to make your game feel real and dynamic with Unity's 2D physics system and animation tools. You'll understand how to animate characters and objects and add visual effects to bring your world to life.
- **Game Design and User Experience**: We'll dive deep into the principles of game design, exploring how to create engaging mechanics, intuitive controls, and a game environment that keeps players coming back for more. From designing levels to balancing difficulty, this book emphasizes user experience.
- **Optimization and Testing**: You'll learn how to optimize your game for performance and how to debug and troubleshoot when things don't go as planned. Understanding optimization early on will

make sure your game runs smoothly across all platforms.

- **Publishing and Beyond**: Once your game is ready, we'll walk you through how to prepare it for release on various platforms, including desktop, mobile, and consoles. You'll also get insights into post-launch support and how to build a community around your game.

A Real-World Approach

Throughout this book, you'll work through a variety of hands-on projects and exercises that illustrate the core concepts of game development in Unity. These aren't abstract or disconnected tasks—everything you learn will build toward your end goal: creating a playable 2D game that you can be proud of. By the end of this book, you'll have gained the knowledge and confidence needed to continue your journey as a game developer, armed with the skills to tackle more complex projects or even start your own game development studio.

This book is designed to be exhaustive, ensuring that you have a comprehensive understanding of Unity and game development. At over 200,000 words, it's not just about following instructions; it's about fully grasping the "why" and "how" of every step, so you can apply this knowledge to your future game projects, no matter how big or small.

Unity's vast capabilities and the depth of game development can sometimes feel overwhelming. But don't worry—you'll have all the guidance you need here. Each chapter is crafted to make complex topics digestible and understandable. Think of it as a step-by-step guide to game development that you can keep going back to for reference as you continue to grow and create.

Start Building Your Dream Game Today

So, are you ready to start building your game? Whether you're looking to develop your first simple platformer, an action-packed shooter, or a narrative-driven adventure, this book will help you make that vision a reality. Let's begin your journey to creating engaging, playable, and memorable games, one step at a time.

This introduction sets the tone for a practical, accessible guide through the Unity game development process, catering to both beginners and experienced developers alike. The goal is to not only teach how to use Unity but also to impart the deeper concepts of game design and development that will help readers create high-quality games.

CHAPTER 1

INTRODUCTION TO UNITY AND GAME DEVELOPMENT BASICS

Overview of Unity: What It Is, Why It's Popular

Unity is a powerful, cross-platform game engine used by developers around the world to create everything from simple mobile games to complex 3D environments and VR experiences. Originally designed for 3D game development, Unity has evolved into one of the most versatile and widely-used game engines, especially for 2D game creation. One of the reasons Unity has become so popular is its accessibility, not only for indie developers but also for major studios.

Unity's core strength lies in its user-friendly interface, a massive library of assets, and its robust support for various platforms—whether you're building a game for PC, consoles, mobile devices, or web browsers. Another huge draw is Unity's scripting language, C#, which is beginner-friendly yet powerful enough for seasoned developers.

Unity provides developers with the tools they need to handle game physics, animations, multiplayer networking, artificial intelligence, and more, all within one engine. Its flexibility allows developers to focus more on creativity rather than wrestling with complex technical details.

Why is Unity popular?

- **Cross-platform support**: Unity can deploy to over 25 platforms, including Windows, macOS, iOS, Android, WebGL, PlayStation, Xbox, and Nintendo Switch.
- **Large community**: With millions of active developers, Unity's community is incredibly resourceful. Whether you're troubleshooting or looking for advice, Unity's forums, tutorials, and asset store have you covered.
- **Rich Asset Store**: The Unity Asset Store offers a huge library of pre-made assets (3D models, animations, sound effects) that developers can use to speed up their projects.
- **Free version available**: Unity offers a free version that includes most of the features you'll need, making it an ideal choice for indie developers and hobbyists.

Understanding the Game Development Lifecycle

Before diving into the technical setup, it's important to understand the process of creating a game. Game development follows a lifecycle that typically goes through several phases, each crucial for producing a polished, functional game. The major phases in the game development lifecycle are:

1. **Concept and Planning**: This is where the game's idea is born. It involves brainstorming game mechanics, storylines, art style, and technical needs. You'll plan your game's features, outline the gameplay, and figure out what technologies are required.
2. **Design**: In this phase, game mechanics are defined. You'll work on level design, art concepts, and the user interface. It's about laying out the blueprint of how the game will work, visually and interactively.
3. **Development/Programming**: The core phase of game creation. Developers write code for the game, which involves building the logic for player movement, interactions, levels, scoring, AI behavior, and more. This is where Unity's scripting tools come into play.
4. **Art and Sound**: Visual assets (characters, backgrounds, animations) and audio elements (sound effects, background music) are created and integrated into the game. The art and sound departments work closely with the developers to ensure that the visuals and audio enhance the gameplay experience.
5. **Testing and Debugging**: Once the game is playable, testing is critical. Developers playtest to identify bugs, glitches, or design flaws that need to be fixed. This process is repeated several times, and each fix or improvement is retested.

6. **Launch**: After extensive testing, the game is ready for release. This phase involves packaging the game for distribution (for example, on the App Store, Google Play, Steam, etc.). Marketing efforts often ramp up around this time.
7. **Post-Launch Support**: After the game is live, the development team may continue to fix bugs, release updates, or add downloadable content (DLC). This phase is essential for keeping the player base engaged and satisfied with the game.

Getting Unity Set Up: Installation and Initial Setup

Before you can start developing, you'll need to install Unity. Unity is compatible with both Windows and macOS, and getting started is straightforward.

1. **Download Unity Hub**: The first step is to download Unity Hub, which is a launcher application that manages Unity installations, projects, and licenses. You can download Unity Hub from Unity's official website: https://unity.com/.
2. **Install Unity Editor**: After installing Unity Hub, you'll need to install the Unity Editor itself. Unity Hub will give you the option to install the latest version of Unity or choose a specific version. For most beginners, the latest stable release is recommended, but if you're working on

a team project or need compatibility with certain assets, you may opt for a different version.

3. **Set Up Your First Project**:
   - Open Unity Hub and click on the "New Project" button.
   - Choose the "2D" template for your game. Unity offers various templates like 2D, 3D, and URP (Universal Render Pipeline), but for this book, we'll stick with the 2D template.
   - Name your project and select a location on your computer to save it.
   - Once you've set up your project, Unity will open the editor, and you'll see an empty scene where you can start creating your game.
4. **Unity Account and License**: If you haven't already, sign up for a Unity account to gain access to the Unity Asset Store, support, and other services. For individual users, Unity offers a free Personal license, as long as your annual revenue from Unity-based projects does not exceed a certain threshold.

Unity Interface: What You Need to Know at the Start

When you first launch Unity, you're presented with a blank project interface that can seem overwhelming. However, once you familiarize yourself with it, it becomes an intuitive tool for game development. Let's go through the key areas of the Unity Editor:

- **Scene View**: This is where you visually design your game. You can drag and drop game objects (like sprites, cameras, and lights) into this window to construct your scenes.
- **Game View**: The Game View window allows you to see how your game will look during playtime. It shows the scene from the camera's perspective, and this is where you test your game while in development.
- **Hierarchy**: The Hierarchy panel lists all the objects in your current scene. Every item, from characters to background elements, will appear here. You can group items together in the hierarchy for easy organization.
- **Inspector**: The Inspector window displays the properties of the currently selected object. Whether you select a sprite, camera, or any other object, the Inspector lets you tweak its attributes (like position, scale, and rotation).
- **Project**: This panel shows all the assets in your project, such as scripts, textures, sounds, and prefabs. Assets can be dragged into your scene from this panel.
- **Console**: The Console displays all of Unity's logs, warnings, and errors. This is where you'll go to troubleshoot issues and track progress while coding.

By the end of this chapter, you should have Unity installed, understand the basics of the Unity interface, and have a firm grasp on the game development lifecycle. Now, you're ready to start building your first game, starting with the foundation that Unity provides.

CHAPTER 2

SETTING UP YOUR FIRST UNITY PROJECT

Starting a 2D Project in Unity

Now that you've installed Unity and familiarized yourself with its interface, it's time to start your first 2D project. Setting up your project correctly from the beginning will save you time later in the development process and help you maintain an organized workflow. Here's how to get started:

1. **Open Unity Hub**: Launch Unity Hub and click on the "New Project" button.
2. **Select the 2D Template**:
    - In Unity Hub, you'll be presented with several templates for different types of projects, such as 2D, 3D, and VR. Since this book is focused on creating a 2D game, choose the "2D" template.
    - Selecting this template automatically sets the default settings and camera for a 2D game (you won't need to worry about setting up 3D features at this stage).
3. **Name Your Project**:

- Give your project a meaningful name. If you're following along with an example, you can name it something like "MyFirst2DGame."
- Choose a location on your computer where the project will be saved. Make sure it's easy to find later.

4. **Create the Project**:
   - Once you've set the project name and location, click the "Create" button. Unity will set up the necessary files and open the editor with an empty scene where you can begin building your game.
5. **Unity's Default Scene**:
   - When your project opens, Unity automatically loads a default scene. This scene is a blank canvas where you can start adding assets and game objects to build your game.

Scene, Game View, and Hierarchy Panel Explained

Once your project is open, the Unity editor will look something like this: the Scene View, Game View, and Hierarchy Panel are the most important sections to familiarize yourself with.

1. **Scene View**:
   - The Scene View is where you design and arrange all the elements of your game. This view lets you

manipulate objects in 2D space, position them, and visually assemble the level or world. You can move, rotate, and scale objects in this view using Unity's tools.

- To navigate around the scene, you can use the right mouse button to look around, hold the middle mouse button to pan, or use the scroll wheel to zoom in and out.
- The Scene View works much like a 2D canvas where you can add and position different game objects—whether they're sprites, cameras, or UI elements.

2. **Game View**:
   - The Game View is where you preview your game while it's running. This is the view that the player will see when they play your game. It displays the scene from the perspective of the camera in the game.
   - In this view, you can test game mechanics, camera angles, and the overall look and feel of your game. It's a great way to simulate gameplay in real time and tweak things before building your final game.
   - You can start and stop the game by pressing the "Play" button at the top of the editor. When you press play, the Game View will show your game

in action, while the Scene View allows you to continue editing the game in real time.

3. **Hierarchy Panel**:
   - The **Hierarchy** panel is a list of all the objects currently present in the scene. Every item in the scene, from your player character to the background, will be listed here. This panel shows the structure of your scene in a way that is easy to navigate.
   - In Unity, every object in the scene is referred to as a "GameObject." A GameObject can represent anything from a sprite (a 2D image) to a light or an invisible piece of code (like a script).
   - You can organize GameObjects in the Hierarchy by grouping them into empty "parent" objects. For example, you could group all the elements of a level into a parent object, which can then be moved or modified together as one entity.
4. **Working with Layers**:
   - The Hierarchy allows you to manage GameObjects in layers. Layers can help you categorize objects and control which objects interact with each other. This can be useful for things like collision detection or controlling visibility for certain objects in specific parts of the game.

- Layers are accessible through the Inspector when selecting a GameObject, allowing you to assign custom labels or functions to different objects in the scene.

Importing Assets and Organizing the Project

Now that you understand the basic views in Unity, it's time to import assets into your project and organize your files. Assets are the building blocks of your game—they include sprites, textures, sounds, animations, scripts, and more. Here's how to import and manage your assets:

1. **Importing Assets**:
   - Unity makes it easy to import assets into your project. To add assets, simply drag them into the Project panel from your file explorer, or go to **Assets > Import New Asset** from the top menu. You can import various file types, including image files (such as PNG or JPEG for sprites), audio files (WAV or MP3), and more.
   - For example, if you have a sprite sheet or individual images for your game, you can drag them into the Project panel and Unity will automatically create textures for you.
2. **Organizing Your Assets**:

- As your project grows, keeping your assets organized becomes essential. Unity offers a **Project** panel, which shows all the assets available in your game.
- Create folders to categorize your assets. Common folders might include:
    - **Sprites**: For all your 2D images, backgrounds, and character sprites.
    - **Audio**: For sound effects and music files.
    - **Scripts**: For C# scripts that control the behavior of your game.
    - **Prefabs**: For reusable objects like buttons, enemies, or obstacles.
    - **Scenes**: For storing your game's different levels or scenes.
- To create a folder, simply right-click in the Project panel and select **Create > Folder**. Naming and organizing your assets early on will help you avoid a cluttered and confusing workspace as your game develops.

3. **Using the Sprite Editor**:
    - If you import a sprite sheet (a single image containing multiple sprites), you can use Unity's **Sprite Editor** to slice the sprite sheet into individual sprites.

  - Select the sprite sheet in the Project panel, then go to the **Inspector** and click on **Sprite Mode**. Choose **Multiple**, and click **Sprite Editor** to slice the image. This allows you to treat each individual sprite as a separate object, making it easier to animate or use in your game.

4. **Creating and Using Prefabs**:
   - Prefabs are reusable templates for game objects. Once you've created an object in your scene, you can drag it into the Project panel to turn it into a prefab. You can then use that prefab across multiple scenes or instances without having to recreate it every time.
   - Prefabs can be useful for common elements like power-ups, enemies, or obstacles that will appear multiple times throughout the game.

By the end of this chapter, you should feel comfortable starting a new 2D Unity project, understanding the key panels and views in the Unity interface, and importing and organizing assets. With this foundation in place, you're now ready to dive into the exciting world of game development!

CHAPTER 3

GAME DESIGN FUNDAMENTALS

Core Principles of Game Design: Mechanics, Dynamics, and Aesthetics

Game design is more than just coding and artwork—it's about creating an experience that resonates with players. At the heart of game design are three fundamental elements: **Mechanics**, **Dynamics**, and **Aesthetics**. These elements work together to define how your game functions, how it engages players, and how it feels to play.

1. **Mechanics**: These are the rules, systems, and basic actions that define how your game operates. Game mechanics dictate how the player interacts with the game world. In a 2D platformer, for example, mechanics would include things like jumping, running, collecting items, or defeating enemies. Mechanics define the "what" of the game—the actions that the player can take.
    - **Examples**:
        - In a puzzle game, the mechanic could be rotating blocks to fit them into a grid.
        - In a fighting game, the mechanic could be combinations of button presses to execute moves.

2. **Dynamics**: Dynamics are the behaviors that emerge as a result of the mechanics interacting with the players and the environment. They refer to how the game mechanics come together in practice and the interactions that result. Dynamics are less about the rules and more about how players engage with those rules.
    - **Example**: In a racing game, the dynamics could include how the vehicle handles on different types of terrain or how the player's actions influence the AI opponents' behavior.
3. **Aesthetics**: Aesthetics are the emotional responses you want to evoke from your players. This encompasses the visual and auditory experience of the game as well as the overall feel of gameplay. The aesthetics also consider the art style, soundtrack, and how the game's atmosphere supports its tone (fun, eerie, suspenseful, etc.).
    - **Example**: A puzzle game may aim for a calm, satisfying aesthetic with soft music and minimalist design. A platformer may aim for an exciting and energetic aesthetic with bright colors and fast-paced music.

These three principles—**mechanics, dynamics, and aesthetics**—form the foundation of every game, whether it's a simple 2D platformer or a complex 3D RPG. Understanding how to balance these elements will be key to making your game both engaging and enjoyable.

Identifying Your Game's Genre

Understanding the genre of your game is crucial for both design and marketing. The genre determines the game's style, rules, mechanics, and often its target audience. Whether you're making a puzzle game, an action game, or a simulation, the genre helps you identify the core aspects of the game and guide the development process.

1. **Common 2D Game Genres**:
    - **Platformers**: These are games where the player moves between platforms, often jumping, avoiding obstacles, and collecting items. Think of classics like *Super Mario Bros.* or *Celeste.*
    - **Puzzle Games**: These games challenge players to solve problems or navigate through intricate levels. *Tetris*, *Candy Crush*, and *Portal* fall into this category.
    - **Shooters**: These focus on combat through shooting mechanics, often involving enemies and weapons. A classic example is *Contra* or *Metal Slug*.
    - **Adventure Games**: These often involve exploration, puzzle-solving, and narrative elements. *The Legend of Zelda* series is a good example.

  - **Roguelikes**: These games typically feature procedurally generated levels and permanent death, where players must start over after losing. *Spelunky* and *Dead Cells* are examples.
  - **Fighting Games**: These involve one-on-one combat between characters, often with different moves and combos. *Street Fighter* and *Mortal Kombat* are iconic in this genre.

2. **Choosing Your Game's Genre**:
  - **Match mechanics to genre**: The genre will directly influence the game mechanics you use. If you're building a platformer, for instance, jumping, running, and avoiding obstacles will likely be part of your core mechanics.
  - **Consider your audience**: Some genres appeal to certain audiences more than others. Puzzle games might appeal to casual gamers, while fighting games might attract players looking for competitive experiences.
  - **Blend genres**: Many successful games mix elements from different genres. For instance, *Metroidvania* games combine platforming with exploration and puzzle-solving. Think about how you can combine genres to create a unique experience.

Once you've identified your game's genre, you'll have a better idea of the gameplay mechanics, level design, and features you'll need to implement. The genre serves as a guiding framework for many of your design decisions.

Game Loop and Player Interaction

The **game loop** is the heart of any game. It's the cycle that repeats throughout the entire gameplay experience, ensuring that the game is engaging and dynamic. The game loop controls how the game responds to player input, updates the game state, and renders the game world.

1. **What is the Game Loop?**
   - The game loop is the process that continuously runs as the game is played. It keeps the game alive by repeating a cycle of actions that update the game state, respond to player input, and render the visuals. It essentially controls the flow of the game, keeping everything in sync.
   - The game loop can be broken down into several stages:
     - **Input Handling**: This is where the game listens for and processes player input, such as keyboard presses or mouse clicks.

- **Game Logic Update**: The game processes the logic, such as character movement, interactions, AI behavior, and the changes in the game world.
- **Rendering**: This is where the game updates what the player sees. It draws the updated game scene to the screen based on the player's actions and game state.
- **Repeat**: The loop then repeats, continuously running until the player stops the game.

In Unity, this loop is primarily handled by Unity's internal functions (like `Update()` and `FixedUpdate()`), but understanding the structure of the loop is essential for writing game code that responds smoothly to player actions.

2. **Player Interaction**:
   - Player interaction refers to how the player interacts with the game world, controls characters, solves puzzles, or engages in combat. How the player engages with the mechanics and dynamics you've designed will determine how enjoyable the game is.
   - **Input Methods**: This could range from keyboard/mouse controls, touch screen input, or

gamepad controllers. Each input method comes with its own challenges and design considerations. For example, on mobile, you might use touch controls, while on a PC, keyboard and mouse input is more typical.

- **Feedback and Rewards**: Good games give players feedback to let them know they're making progress. This can come in the form of sound effects, visual cues (like animations or flashing lights), or even score systems. Rewards, such as leveling up, unlocking new abilities, or gaining points, help keep players motivated.
- **Player Challenges**: A good game provides challenges that are difficult but not impossible. It should push the player to improve, but not frustrate them to the point of quitting. Balancing difficulty is an art in itself.

Bringing It All Together

In this chapter, you've learned the foundational principles of game design: **mechanics**, **dynamics**, and **aesthetics**. By combining these three elements thoughtfully, you can create an engaging and enjoyable game experience. Additionally, understanding your game's genre will help define its core mechanics and target audience, ensuring your game is both fun and accessible.

Finally, we explored the **game loop**—the repetitive cycle that powers every game. Understanding this will allow you to write the code that keeps your game responsive and interactive. When done right, the game loop and player interaction create an immersive and compelling experience for players.

With this knowledge in hand, you're ready to move forward and begin building your 2D game in Unity, applying these principles to make your game engaging, challenging, and most importantly—fun!

CHAPTER 4

UNITY'S 2D SYSTEM: GETTING STARTED

Unity 2D Workflows and Tools

Unity's 2D system is specifically designed to help developers create engaging 2D games with ease. Whether you're building a platformer, a puzzle game, or a top-down adventure, Unity's 2D tools and workflows are essential to bringing your vision to life. In this section, we'll cover the primary tools and workflows you'll use when working in a 2D environment.

1. **Setting Up for 2D Development**:
   - Before you dive into building your 2D game, ensure that your Unity project is set up correctly. In the previous chapter, you learned how to start a new 2D project. But it's important to know what's different in 2D development.
   - **Camera Setup**: By default, Unity sets the camera to **Orthographic** mode when you create a 2D project. This ensures that objects appear at the same size regardless of their distance from the camera, which is essential for 2D games.

- **Scene Setup**: When you're working with 2D, you'll mostly be arranging objects in a 2D plane (X and Y axis). Unity's 2D view mode helps you focus on this plane, making it easier to position, move, and align objects.

2. **Using the Scene View and Game View**:
   - **Scene View**: In Unity, the Scene View is where you design the world of your game. For 2D projects, the Scene View lets you see your objects from a top-down view, with a focus on the X and Y axes. You'll use the Scene View to place and move sprites, adjust their properties, and set up the game world.
   - **Game View**: This is where you test your game. While the Scene View shows the layout of objects, the Game View simulates how the player will see the game when it's running. This is where you'll see the results of your game's mechanics, animations, and interactions.
3. **Tilemaps and Grid System**:
   - **Tilemaps** are one of Unity's most powerful tools for 2D game development, especially when creating platformers or top-down games. Unity's **Tilemap system** allows you to paint large levels using individual tiles, creating a grid-based map for your game.

- You can create **Tile Palette** and use it to organize and paint tiles on your Tilemap. The Tilemap system works seamlessly with Unity's 2D physics and lighting system, so you can create intricate levels that interact with the player and game world.

4. **Unity's Sprite Renderer**:
   - The **Sprite Renderer** is the component used to display 2D images (sprites) in Unity. Each GameObject that you want to be displayed as a 2D image must have a Sprite Renderer attached. You can assign any sprite to this renderer through the Inspector.
   - The Sprite Renderer allows you to control the position, rotation, scale, and color of your sprites in the game world. You can also adjust how sprites interact with the camera, such as their sorting order (layering) to control which sprite appears in front or behind others.

Working with Sprites and Animating Them

Sprites are the building blocks of 2D games, representing characters, objects, backgrounds, and other visual elements. Unity makes it easy to work with sprites and animate them for fluid character movements or interactive environments.

1. **Importing and Using Sprites**:
   - Sprites can be imported into Unity as individual image files (PNG, JPG, etc.), which are then displayed on GameObjects. To import a sprite, simply drag and drop the image file into Unity's **Project Panel**. Unity automatically recognizes the image as a sprite if the file's texture type is set to **Sprite (2D and UI)** in the Inspector.
   - Once you have a sprite in your project, create a new GameObject and attach the Sprite Renderer component to display it. From the Inspector, assign the imported sprite to the Renderer's **Sprite** field.
2. **Creating Animations with Sprites**:
   - Unity allows you to create 2D animations by switching between different sprites over time. For example, if you have a character with a series of walking sprites, you can animate them by creating an **Animation Clip**.
   - To create an animation:
     - Select your sprite or sprite-based GameObject in the scene.
     - Open the **Animation Window** (Window > Animation > Animation).

        - Click **Create** to make a new animation clip. Unity will prompt you to save the clip in the Project panel.
        - Add keyframes for your animation by dragging sprites from the Project panel into the Timeline in the Animation window. Unity will automatically interpolate between these keyframes to create smooth transitions.
        - You can set the speed, loop, and timing of the animation in the Animator Controller, which allows for complex state machines and transitions between different animations.

3. **Animator Controller**:
    - The **Animator Controller** is responsible for managing all of a GameObject's animations. It allows you to set up a state machine, which lets your character switch between different animations based on game events. For example, you could set up animations for walking, jumping, and idle states.
    - You can connect different animations and set up transitions between them using conditions such as player input, character speed, or other game variables.

4. **Animating with the Sprite Renderer**:
   - Besides the full Animation system, you can also animate a sprite directly using the Sprite Renderer. This is useful for simple animations or sprite-based effects, like an object changing color or flickering.
   - You can use scripts to change the sprite displayed by the Sprite Renderer at runtime. For example, a script can cycle through sprites to create a walking animation by switching between frames of a character's walk cycle.

The Importance of Sprite Sheets

In 2D game development, **sprite sheets** are often used to efficiently organize and store multiple sprites on a single image. Instead of importing each sprite individually, you can pack them together in one large image, which reduces the number of assets you need to manage and improves performance.

1. **What is a Sprite Sheet?**
   - A sprite sheet is a single image file that contains multiple frames of a character animation or other repeated visual elements. For example, instead of having separate files for each frame of a

character's walk cycle, you can combine them all into one image.

- The sprite sheet can contain several different animations, such as idle, walking, and jumping, with each row or column of the sheet representing a different animation sequence.

2. **Importing and Slicing Sprite Sheets**:
   - To work with sprite sheets in Unity, you first import them as a single image file. Then, you use Unity's **Sprite Editor** to slice the sprite sheet into individual sprites.
     - Select the sprite sheet in the Project panel, and in the Inspector, change the **Sprite Mode** to **Multiple**.
     - Click the **Sprite Editor** button to open the editor, where you can manually slice the sheet into individual sprites or let Unity automatically slice it based on your grid settings.
     - After slicing, you can drag the individual sprites into your scene or use them in animations.
3. **Benefits of Using Sprite Sheets**:
   - **Performance**: Using sprite sheets can improve the performance of your game. Instead of loading multiple image files, Unity can load and display

all the sprites from a single sheet, reducing the overhead of multiple file accesses.

- **Organization**: Sprite sheets make it easier to keep your assets organized. Instead of hunting through several image files, you can manage all the related sprites in one place.
- **Consistency**: When you use a sprite sheet for animations, you can ensure that all frames are perfectly aligned and have a consistent look. This helps maintain the visual continuity of your game.

4. **Optimizing Sprite Sheets**:
   - Keep an eye on the size of your sprite sheets. Very large sprite sheets can use a lot of memory and potentially slow down performance, especially on mobile platforms.
   - You can reduce the file size by compressing images or using **sprite packing**, which allows Unity to group multiple sprite sheets together into a single texture atlas.

Summary

In this chapter, you've learned about Unity's 2D tools and workflows, which are essential for creating 2D games. You now understand how to set up your project for 2D development, work with sprites, and animate them using Unity's powerful animation system. You've also explored the concept of sprite sheets, which can help you optimize performance and keep your assets organized.

With these tools in hand, you're ready to start building the visual aspects of your 2D game, adding character animations, creating dynamic interactions, and fine-tuning the game's aesthetics. The next steps will involve deeper dives into game mechanics, level design, and other gameplay elements that will bring your project to life.

CHAPTER 5

PHYSICS AND COLLISIONS IN UNITY

Introduction to Unity's 2D Physics Engine

Unity's 2D physics engine is a powerful tool that allows you to simulate realistic interactions between objects in your game world. By incorporating physics into your 2D games, you can create more immersive and dynamic gameplay experiences. Unity uses **Box2D**, an open-source 2D physics engine, to handle things like collisions, gravity, and forces in a 2D space. The 2D physics engine is specifically optimized for 2D games, making it lighter and more efficient than 3D physics systems.

In Unity, the 2D physics engine is integrated into the **Physics 2D** module, which is responsible for handling all physics-based calculations, including collisions, forces, and movement of 2D objects.

1. **Core Physics Concepts**:
   - **Collisions**: Unity uses colliders to detect when two objects come into contact. A collision might cause a response, such as bouncing, sliding, or triggering an event in the game.

- **Forces**: Forces such as gravity, friction, and applied forces can influence the movement of objects in your game world. These forces can be simulated to make objects move in a realistic or dramatic way.
- **Rigidbodies**: A Rigidbody is a component that allows an object to be affected by physics. By attaching a Rigidbody to a GameObject, Unity will handle the object's movement, collisions, and forces.

Setting Up Colliders for Interaction

Colliders are the key components in Unity that handle detecting whether two objects are touching or intersecting. They don't directly affect the visual representation of the object, but they define the area that can interact with other objects, either by colliding or triggering events.

1. **Types of Colliders**: Unity offers a variety of 2D colliders, each suited for different shapes and types of interaction:
    - **Box Collider 2D**: This is the most common collider and works well for rectangular or square shapes. It's a simple box that covers the GameObject's bounds.

- **Circle Collider 2D**: Used for circular or round objects. This collider is best suited for round characters or objects.
- **Polygon Collider 2D**: Used for irregularly shaped objects. This collider allows you to define a custom shape for collisions.
- **Edge Collider 2D**: Best for creating line-based collisions, such as for platforms or thin objects like wires or beams.
- **Composite Collider 2D**: Used for combining multiple colliders (usually attached to the same GameObject) into a single collider. This is especially useful when your object has several separate colliders but you want them to behave as one cohesive shape.

2. **Setting Up a Collider**:
   - To add a collider to a GameObject, select the object in the **Hierarchy** window, then click **Add Component** in the Inspector panel. Search for the collider you want to add (Box Collider 2D, Circle Collider 2D, etc.) and select it.
   - After adding the collider, Unity will automatically generate the collider shape around your GameObject's sprite. You can adjust the size and position of the collider using the **Collider's properties** in the Inspector.

- You can also adjust the **Is Trigger** option for the collider. If this option is checked, the collider will only detect when other objects pass through it but won't cause physical collisions. This is useful for triggering events (e.g., picking up an item).

3. **Collisions and Triggers**:
    - **Collisions**: When two colliders come into contact, Unity will trigger a collision event. The objects will physically respond based on their Rigidbody settings (we'll discuss this in the next section). For example, objects may stop, bounce off one another, or slide depending on how you configure them.
    - **Triggers**: When the **Is Trigger** checkbox is checked, the collider will not physically interact with other objects (no bounce or stopping), but it will still send notifications that something has entered or exited the area. Triggers are useful for creating events like opening doors, collecting items, or causing enemies to take damage.

Understanding Rigidbodies and Gravity in 2D Games

Rigidbodies are the key to allowing GameObjects to react to Unity's physics system. They provide objects with mass, drag, and other physical properties that define how they behave under forces and collisions.

1. **Adding a Rigidbody 2D**:
   - A **Rigidbody 2D** is added to a GameObject to allow it to be influenced by the 2D physics engine. You can add a Rigidbody 2D to your object by selecting it in the **Hierarchy**, clicking **Add Component** in the Inspector, and choosing **Rigidbody 2D**.
   - Once added, the Rigidbody 2D enables physics-based behaviors such as movement, gravity, and collisions. The Rigidbody 2D interacts with other objects based on their colliders and the forces applied to it.
2. **Rigidbody 2D Properties**:
   - **Mass**: Determines how much force is needed to move the object. Larger masses require more force to accelerate.
   - **Gravity Scale**: Controls how strongly the object is affected by gravity. A value of 1 means it will be affected by gravity normally. A value of 0 means it will not be affected by gravity at all, making the object float. You can adjust this value to create gravity effects tailored to your game.

- **Drag**: This simulates air resistance. The higher the drag, the slower an object will move over time, making it feel heavier.
- **Angular Drag**: Affects how quickly the object's rotation slows down. This is useful for objects that rotate, such as spinning blades or wheels.
- **Use Auto Mass**: This automatically calculates the mass of an object based on its size and type. While this is convenient, you can manually adjust the mass to suit the gameplay mechanics.

3. **Gravity in 2D Games**:
   - Gravity is one of the most fundamental forces in any physics-based game, especially in platformers or games with characters who jump or fall.
   - Unity applies gravity to all GameObjects that have a Rigidbody 2D attached. The default gravity value in Unity is set in the **Physics 2D settings** (Edit > Project Settings > Physics 2D), and it typically applies a downward force along the Y-axis. However, you can adjust the gravity scale for individual objects to make some objects more or less affected by gravity.
   - To simulate different gravity effects, you could set the gravity scale for certain objects to a low value, allowing them to float or move more

slowly. For example, in a puzzle game, you might have objects that defy gravity or float upwards.

4. **Applying Forces to Rigidbodies**:
   - You can apply forces to a Rigidbody 2D to move or propel it in the game world. This can be done through **AddForce**, **AddTorque**, or setting the **velocity** directly. Forces are essential for simulating things like pushing objects, jumping, or creating momentum.
   - **AddForce** applies an external force to the object and can be used for things like launching a character or throwing an object. You can adjust the direction, magnitude, and force type (such as **impulse** or **force**).
   - **AddTorque** adds rotational force to an object, causing it to spin. This is great for creating rotating objects or vehicles.

Summary

In this chapter, we've explored how to use Unity's 2D physics engine to bring dynamic and interactive elements into your game. You've learned about the different types of colliders and how to set them up for object interactions. Additionally, we discussed

Rigidbody 2D components, which make your objects respond to forces and gravity, creating realistic physical behavior.

By mastering the basics of physics and collisions in Unity, you can create engaging gameplay elements like character movement, environmental interactions, and realistic object behaviors. Whether you're designing platformers, puzzle games, or action adventures, understanding Unity's 2D physics engine will be essential for creating fun and engaging experiences for your players.

CHAPTER 6

SCRIPTING IN UNITY (C# BASICS)

Introduction to C# Scripting in Unity

Scripting is one of the core aspects of game development in Unity. It's through scripts that you bring the logic, interaction, and mechanics of your game to life. Unity uses **C#** as its primary programming language, which is powerful, flexible, and widely used across the game development industry. C# offers a robust set of features, making it an excellent choice for scripting in Unity.

In this chapter, we'll introduce the basics of scripting in Unity using C#. You'll learn how to write simple scripts, implement basic player controls, and understand how Unity handles scripts through the **MonoBehaviour** class and its event methods.

Writing Simple Scripts: Moving an Object, Player Controls

To begin writing scripts in Unity, we first need to understand how to create and attach them to GameObjects. Scripts in Unity are typically written in **Visual Studio** or **Rider**, which are integrated with Unity to provide helpful features like code completion, error checking, and debugging.

1. **Creating a Script**:
   - In Unity, you can create a new script by right-clicking in the **Project** window, navigating to **Create > C# Script**, and giving it a meaningful name (e.g., "PlayerController").
   - Once the script is created, double-click it to open it in your chosen code editor (usually Visual Studio). This will open up a default script template with a **MonoBehaviour** class.
2. **Basic Script Structure**: Every script in Unity starts with the **MonoBehaviour** class. The class contains two essential methods, **Start()** and **Update()**, that are automatically called by Unity during the game's runtime.

```
csharp
CopyEdit
using UnityEngine;

public class PlayerController :
MonoBehaviour
{
    // Variables for movement speed
    public float moveSpeed = 5f;

    // Called once when the game starts
    void Start()
    {
        // Initialize things here
```

```
    }

    // Called once per frame
    void Update()
    {
        // Handle player input for movement
        MovePlayer();
    }

    void MovePlayer()
    {
        //   Get   horizontal   and   vertical
input (WASD or Arrow keys)
        float          moveX          =
Input.GetAxis("Horizontal");
        float          moveY          =
Input.GetAxis("Vertical");

        // Move the player using the input
values
        transform.Translate(new
Vector3(moveX,  moveY,  0)  *  moveSpeed  *
Time.deltaTime);
    }
}
```

- **Variables**: In this example, we declare a public variable `moveSpeed`, which will control how fast the player moves. Public variables can be adjusted in the Unity **Inspector**.

- **Start()**: The **Start()** method is called once when the script is first executed. You can use it to initialize any variables or setup.
- **Update()**: The **Update()** method is called every frame, which makes it the ideal place for handling player input, movement, or other time-sensitive operations.
- **MovePlayer()**: This is a custom method we created to handle player movement. It uses Unity's **Input.GetAxis()** method to detect horizontal and vertical input from the player (e.g., arrow keys, WASD).

3. **Attaching the Script to a GameObject**:
    - After writing your script, save the changes and return to Unity. To attach the script to a GameObject (like the player character), simply drag the script from the **Project** window onto the GameObject in the **Hierarchy** window. Alternatively, you can select the GameObject, click **Add Component** in the Inspector, and search for your script by name.
    - Once the script is attached, Unity will automatically run it during gameplay, and any

public variables (like `moveSpeed`) will be visible and adjustable in the Inspector.

4. **Player Movement**: The `MovePlayer()` function uses the **Translate()** method to move the player GameObject. This method moves the object by a given vector (in this case, the movement input from the player). **Time.deltaTime** ensures that the movement speed is consistent regardless of the frame rate.

Understanding the MonoBehaviour Class and Unity's Event Methods

In Unity, scripts are based on the **MonoBehaviour** class, which provides a set of built-in methods that are automatically called by Unity. These methods are crucial for managing how objects behave during different phases of the game.

1. **MonoBehaviour Overview**:
   - **MonoBehaviour** is the base class from which every Unity script derives. When you create a new script, Unity automatically extends **MonoBehaviour** in that script, giving you access to Unity's event functions like **Start()**, **Update()**, and others.

- A **MonoBehaviour** script is tied to a GameObject in the scene, and each script can be attached to one or more GameObjects.

2. **Common MonoBehaviour Methods**:
   - **Start()**: Called when the script is first initialized, before any update calls. It's a great place to set initial values or perform one-time setup tasks. It is called once during the game's lifecycle.
   - **Update()**: Called once per frame. This is where most of your game logic and updates will take place. It's ideal for handling input, checking conditions, and updating object positions or properties.
   - **FixedUpdate()**: Similar to **Update()**, but called at a fixed interval, making it ideal for physics calculations and Rigidbody-based movements. This ensures more consistent and predictable behavior for physics interactions.
   - **LateUpdate()**: Called after all **Update()** methods have been called. It's useful for scenarios where you want to ensure that the camera or other objects update after the main game logic has run.
   - **Awake()**: Called when the script instance is being loaded. It's used for initialization tasks that need to occur before the game begins or before the script is activated.

- **OnCollisionEnter2D()**, **OnTriggerEnter2D()**: These methods are used for detecting collisions and triggers between GameObjects. **OnCollisionEnter2D()** is called when two non-trigger colliders collide, while **OnTriggerEnter2D()** is called when a collider set to "Trigger" enters another collider.
- **OnDestroy()**: Called when the object to which the script is attached is destroyed or deactivated. This method is helpful for cleaning up resources or stopping background processes.

3. **Using Unity's Event Methods**:
    - Unity's built-in event methods (such as **Start()**, **Update()**, and **Awake()**) help developers manage the timing of operations. These methods are automatically triggered by Unity at the appropriate points in the game's lifecycle. Understanding when and how these methods are called can be crucial for writing efficient and bug-free code.
    - For example, if you want an object to start moving when the game begins, you would write that logic in the **Start()** method. If you want to continuously check for user input, you would do that in **Update()**.

  - Event-driven programming in Unity means that certain actions or conditions will automatically call the appropriate methods based on the game's state (such as object collisions, input, or frame updates).

Debugging and Testing Scripts

1. **Debugging in Unity**:
   - Debugging is an essential part of game development. Unity provides a powerful **Debug** class that allows you to print information to the console for troubleshooting.
   - For example, you can use `Debug.Log()` to print messages to the Unity console. This is helpful for checking if certain parts of your script are being executed.

```
csharp
CopyEdit
void Update()
{
    float moveX = Input.GetAxis("Horizontal");
    Debug.Log("Moving horizontally: " + moveX);
}
```

2. **Using Breakpoints**:
    - You can also use breakpoints and the built-in debugger in Visual Studio to step through your code line-by-line and observe how variables change during runtime. This allows you to catch logical errors or unexpected behavior in your game's scripts.

Summary

In this chapter, you've learned the basics of scripting in Unity using C#. We covered how to create scripts, move objects with basic player controls, and interact with Unity's event methods through the **MonoBehaviour** class. By understanding the fundamental Unity scripting methods like **Start()**, **Update()**, and **FixedUpdate()**, you can create smooth and responsive gameplay experiences.

Scripting is a powerful tool in your game development toolkit, and as you advance, you'll write more complex and interactive scripts. The next steps will include learning how to add more dynamic behaviors to your game, such as handling player input, managing game states, and working with animations and sound.

CHAPTER 7

HANDLING PLAYER INPUT

Detecting User Input: Keyboard, Mouse, and Touch Input

One of the most important aspects of game development is how the player interacts with the game world. Handling input is essential to allowing players to control characters, interact with objects, and influence the game in real time. Unity provides several built-in ways to detect and process input from different devices, including the keyboard, mouse, and touchscreens.

1. **Keyboard Input**: The most common form of input in many games is from the keyboard. Unity makes it easy to detect which keys are pressed using the **Input.GetKey()**, **Input.GetKeyDown()**, and **Input.GetKeyUp()** methods. These allow you to check whether a key is being held down, pressed once, or released.
    - **Input.GetKey()**: Checks if a particular key is being held down.
    - **Input.GetKeyDown()**: Checks if a key was pressed in the current frame.
    - **Input.GetKeyUp()**: Checks if a key was released in the current frame.

Example: Moving a character left and right using the arrow keys or WASD:

```
csharp
CopyEdit
void Update()
{
    float moveX = 0f;

    if (Input.GetKey(KeyCode.A))    // Move
left
    {
        moveX = -1f;
    }
    if (Input.GetKey(KeyCode.D))    // Move
right
    {
        moveX = 1f;
    }

    transform.Translate(new Vector3(moveX,
0, 0) * moveSpeed * Time.deltaTime);
}
```

2. **Mouse Input**: The mouse is another common input device, especially for games with point-and-click mechanics or camera control. Unity offers several methods for detecting mouse input.

- **Input.GetMouseButton()**: Returns true while the mouse button is held down (useful for drag interactions).
- **Input.GetMouseButtonDown()**: Returns true only during the frame the mouse button is pressed.
- **Input.GetMouseButtonUp()**: Returns true only during the frame the mouse button is released.
- **Input.mousePosition**: Gives you the current position of the mouse cursor on the screen in pixel coordinates.

Example: Detecting mouse clicks and moving a GameObject towards the mouse position:

```
csharp
CopyEdit
void Update()
{
    if (Input.GetMouseButtonDown(0))    //
Left-click
    {
        Vector3      mousePosition      =
Camera.main.ScreenToWorldPoint(Input.mous
ePosition);
        mousePosition.z = 0;  // Ensure the
Z-axis is 0 for 2D games
```

```
        transform.position =
mousePosition;
    }
}
```

- The **ScreenToWorldPoint** method converts the screen space coordinates of the mouse to world space, which allows us to move the GameObject based on the mouse's position in the game scene.

3. **Touch Input** (for mobile games): Unity also supports touch input, which is vital for mobile game development. Touch input is similar to mouse input, but it involves multi-touch gestures, swipes, taps, and more.
   - **Input.touchCount**: Returns the number of active touches on the screen.
   - **Input.GetTouch()**: Returns information about each touch (e.g., position, delta, phase).

Example: Detecting a simple touch and moving a character accordingly:

```
csharp
CopyEdit
void Update()
{
    if (Input.touchCount > 0)  // Check if
there is at least one touch
    {
```

```
            Touch  touch  =  Input.GetTouch(0);
// Get the first touch
            Vector3      touchPosition       =
Camera.main.ScreenToWorldPoint(touch.posi
tion);
            touchPosition.z = 0;  // Ensure the
Z-axis is 0 for 2D games
            transform.position               =
touchPosition;
        }
}
```

The **Input.touchCount** checks how many touches are active, and **Input.GetTouch(0)** retrieves information about the first touch. **touch.position** provides the position of the touch on the screen, which is then converted to world coordinates using **ScreenToWorldPoint**.

Implementing Character Movement Controls

Now that we've covered how to detect input from different sources, let's implement responsive character movement. Character movement is one of the most fundamental gameplay elements, and Unity provides different ways to handle it.

1. **Using the Keyboard for Movement**: The most straightforward way to implement movement is by

detecting key presses and moving the character based on the input. This was demonstrated in the previous example where the player moved left and right using the arrow keys or WASD.

To implement **smooth movement**, we can add some velocity to the movement system and handle player input more fluidly:

```
csharp
CopyEdit
public float moveSpeed = 5f;
public float moveSmoothness = 0.1f;
private Vector3 velocity = Vector3.zero;

void Update()
{
    float                    moveX              =
Input.GetAxis("Horizontal");      //   Gets
input from arrow keys or WASD
    float                    moveY              =
Input.GetAxis("Vertical");

    Vector3     targetMovement     =     new
Vector3(moveX, moveY, 0);
    transform.position                          =
Vector3.SmoothDamp(transform.position,
transform.position  +  targetMovement,  ref
velocity, moveSmoothness);
```

```
}
```

- Input.GetAxis() automatically handles input smoothing and works for both keyboard and controller inputs (if available).
- The **Vector3.SmoothDamp** method is used to gradually move the character to the target position, creating smooth transitions.

2. **Using Rigidbody2D for Movement**: For more advanced movement, particularly when working with physics (e.g., for jumps or interactions with objects), it's better to use Unity's **Rigidbody2D** component. This allows you to move objects using physics forces like **AddForce()** or by directly setting the **velocity** of the Rigidbody.

   Example: Using a Rigidbody2D to move a character with keyboard input:

```
csharp
CopyEdit
public float moveSpeed = 5f;
private Rigidbody2D rb;

void Start()
{
    rb = GetComponent<Rigidbody2D>();    //
Get the Rigidbody2D component
}
```

```
void Update()
{
    float                    moveX                    =
Input.GetAxis("Horizontal");
    float                    moveY                    =
Input.GetAxis("Vertical");

    rb.velocity = new Vector2(moveX *
moveSpeed, moveY * moveSpeed);
}
```

- **Rigidbody2D.velocity** directly controls the object's velocity, and we use **Input.GetAxis()** for continuous movement. This ensures that the character reacts to the physics engine.

3. **Jumping and Gravity**: If you want to implement jumping, you can combine **Rigidbody2D** with forces to make the character jump when the player presses a button. Here's how to add a basic jump mechanic:

```
csharp
CopyEdit
public float moveSpeed = 5f;
public float jumpForce = 5f;
private Rigidbody2D rb;
private bool isGrounded;

void Start()
```

```
{
    rb = GetComponent<Rigidbody2D>();
}

void Update()
{
    float moveX =
Input.GetAxis("Horizontal");
    rb.velocity = new Vector2(moveX *
moveSpeed, rb.velocity.y); // Horizontal
movement

    if (isGrounded &&
Input.GetKeyDown(KeyCode.Space)) // Jump
on space bar press
    {
        rb.AddForce(Vector2.up *
jumpForce, ForceMode2D.Impulse);
    }
}

void OnCollisionEnter2D(Collision2D other)
{
    if
(other.gameObject.CompareTag("Ground"))
// Check if the player is on the ground
    {
        isGrounded = true;
    }
```

```
}

void OnCollisionExit2D(Collision2D other)
{
    if
(other.gameObject.CompareTag("Ground"))
    {
        isGrounded = false;
    }
}
```

- The **jumpForce** is applied using **AddForce()**, and we check if the player is grounded using a collision check with the ground. The **isGrounded** boolean ensures that the player can only jump when they are on the ground, preventing double jumps in mid-air.

Building Responsive Game Mechanics

To build responsive game mechanics, it's important that player controls feel immediate and natural. Here are a few tips for building responsive gameplay:

1. **Input Sensitivity**: When detecting input, ensure that there is a balance between responsiveness and control. For example, instead of moving the character one unit per

frame, you could use **Input.GetAxis()** for smooth movement that adjusts based on the input intensity, making the controls more fluid.

2. **Acceleration and Deceleration**: Implementing acceleration and deceleration can make movement feel more natural. For example, the player could gradually speed up when moving and slow down when stopping, rather than instantly changing direction.
3. **Input Buffering**: In some games, especially action titles, input buffering allows players to queue up actions like jumping or attacking slightly before pressing the button, making the game feel more responsive. This ensures that the player's actions are detected even if they press the button at the wrong moment.
4. **Feedback and Animation**: Providing visual or audio feedback when the player interacts with the game world (like a character jumping or landing) increases immersion. For example, you might trigger an animation whenever the player moves or jumps, making the input feel more connected to the character's actions.

Summary

In this chapter, we've covered the basics of handling player input in Unity using the keyboard, mouse, and touch devices. We've walked through examples for detecting input and implementing responsive character controls using Unity's **Input** system. We also explored using **Rigidbody2D** for physics-based movement, adding jumping mechanics, and making the game feel responsive through input sensitivity and acceleration. Understanding how to manage player input effectively is key to creating engaging and fun gameplay experiences.

CHAPTER 8

CREATING THE GAME ENVIRONMENT

Creating the game environment is an essential part of game development, as it provides the context and setting where your gameplay unfolds. A well-designed environment not only enhances the visual appeal of your game but also significantly impacts gameplay by guiding player movement, creating challenges, and reinforcing the story or theme.

In this chapter, we'll explore how to design simple levels, add background and foreground elements, and use Unity's Tilemap system for 2D level creation.

Designing Simple Levels

When designing game levels, the primary goal is to create an engaging environment that is fun to play in and complements the game's mechanics. Here are some key considerations:

1. **Player Flow**: Think about how players will navigate through your levels. Are there obstacles? Is there a clear path to follow, or should the player explore? A well-

designed level should guide the player naturally through the game world while keeping them engaged.

- **Linear levels**: These levels have a clear starting point and an endpoint. They work well for games where progression is important.
- **Non-linear levels**: These allow players to explore and find their own path. Think of games like Metroidvania, where exploration and discovery are key to progression.

2. **Challenges and Obstacles**: Levels should provide a balance between challenges and rewards. Adding obstacles (like pits, enemies, or puzzles) encourages the player to think about how they navigate the level. Use your level design to teach the player about game mechanics and gradually introduce new challenges.
3. **Spacing**: Pay attention to the spacing between obstacles and platforms. Make sure that areas are neither too crowded nor too empty. Tight spaces can create intense challenges, while too much open space can make the level feel boring.
4. **Theme and Style**: The design of your levels should reflect the theme and style of your game. Whether you're building a medieval castle or a futuristic city, the layout of your levels and the placement of objects should support the overall aesthetic.

Adding Background and Foreground Elements

The background and foreground elements of your game help set the scene and create depth, making your game world feel more immersive. Unity allows you to easily layer different graphical elements to create a sense of perspective and atmosphere.

1. **Background Elements**: The background often serves to establish the mood and setting of the level without distracting from the player's actions. These elements are typically static but can be animated or parallax-scrolled to add more dynamism.
    - **Static backgrounds**: These are usually simple images or patterns that remain in place while the player moves through the level. For example, you could have a distant mountain range or a sunset sky in the background.
    - **Parallax scrolling**: This technique involves moving background elements at different speeds to create a sense of depth. For instance, closer objects (like trees or clouds) move faster than objects in the distance (like mountains), making the world feel more three-dimensional.
2. **Foreground Elements**: Foreground elements, such as trees, rocks, or signs, help enhance the player's interaction with the environment. These elements can be used to obscure certain parts of the screen, providing

opportunities for design challenges or creating a sense of immersion.

- **Obstacles and covers**: Foreground elements can also be interactive, like walls the player can hide behind or obstacles they need to jump over. These elements are designed to impact the player's movement and interaction with the environment.
- **Visual interest**: Using foreground elements strategically adds richness to the environment. For example, placing trees or buildings in the foreground can provide additional texture to a level without overwhelming the player.

3. **Layering**: The key to effectively using both background and foreground elements is to layer them. Unity's **sorting layers** feature allows you to manage the visual stacking order of objects, ensuring that some elements appear in front of or behind others. This feature is essential when creating a multi-layered 2D environment.

Using Tilemaps and Unity's Tilemap System for 2D Level Creation

Unity's **Tilemap system** is a powerful tool for creating 2D game environments, especially for games with grid-based layouts. It allows you to design large, efficient levels quickly by painting tiles onto a grid.

Here's how to get started with Tilemaps in Unity:

1. **Setting Up the Tilemap System**: First, you need to set up the Tilemap system in Unity. This is done by creating a **Tilemap** object in your scene.
    - In the **Hierarchy** window, right-click and go to **2D Object** > **Tilemap** > **Rectangular** (or any other Tilemap type, like Isometric or Hexagonal).
    - This will create a new **Grid** object with a **Tilemap** child. The Grid component determines how the tiles are arranged in your scene, and the Tilemap holds the actual tiles.
2. **Creating and Importing Tiles**: Tiles are the building blocks of your level. You can create your own tiles by importing sprite images (such as ground, platforms, or walls) into Unity. Once imported, you can turn them into tiles that you can use on the Tilemap.
    - **Importing tiles**: To import tiles, simply drag and drop image files (like PNGs) into your **Assets** folder.
    - **Creating tile assets**: Right-click in the **Assets** window, go to **Create** > **Tile** to create a new Tile asset. Then, assign the corresponding sprite to it by dragging the sprite from the **Assets** into the **Tile** inspector.
3. **Painting the Level**: With your Tilemap and Tiles set up, you can now begin painting your level. Unity provides an

intuitive **Tile Palette** window where you can drag and drop tiles from your **Assets** to quickly paint them onto the Tilemap in the Scene view.

- **Tile Palette**: Open the **Tile Palette** window (Window > 2D > Tile Palette), then drag your tiles from the **Assets** into the palette.
- Use the brush tool in the Tile Palette to start painting tiles onto your Tilemap. You can easily adjust the size of the brush, the shape of tiles, and even use special tools like the **Fill** tool to paint large areas quickly.

4. **Collision with Tiles**: Unity allows you to add **Tilemap Colliders** to your Tilemap, which automatically detects collisions with the tiles. This is useful for creating walkable surfaces or obstacles without needing to manually place individual colliders on each tile.
   - To add a collider, simply select your **Tilemap** object and click **Add Component** > **Tilemap Collider 2D**. This will add a collider to every tile that interacts with physics.
   - You can also use **Composite Collider 2D** in combination with the Tilemap Collider for more efficient collision detection, as it combines multiple individual colliders into a single, optimized collider.

5. **Adding Tilemap Layers**: In many games, you'll want to use multiple Tilemaps to create layers for your level, such as a ground layer, a background layer, and a foreground layer. By stacking multiple Tilemap objects, you can build a more dynamic environment.
    - **Layering Tilemaps**: Simply create additional Tilemaps in the same Grid object. Each Tilemap can represent a different layer, and you can control their sorting order using the **Order in Layer** property to determine what appears in front or behind other layers.
6. **Animating Tiles**: You can animate tiles to create dynamic elements in your environment, such as moving platforms or pulsing lights. To animate a tile, you can create a **Tilemap Animation**.
    - **Tilemap Animation**: Right-click on a Tile in the **Tile Palette** and select **Create > Animation Clip**. This allows you to sequence different tiles over time to create an animated effect.

Summary

In this chapter, we've explored the process of creating a game environment using Unity. Starting with designing simple levels, we covered the importance of player flow, challenges, and theme consistency. We also looked at how to enhance the environment with background and foreground elements to create a more immersive game world.

The chapter concluded with an introduction to Unity's Tilemap system, a powerful tool for efficiently creating 2D game levels. By utilizing Tilemaps, you can paint your levels, add collision detection, layer elements, and even animate tiles to bring your environment to life. Mastering the Tilemap system is crucial for creating large, structured game environments with minimal effort.

CHAPTER 9

ADDING OBSTACLES AND ENEMIES

In any game, obstacles and enemies are central to providing challenge and engagement for players. They add tension, excitement, and a sense of accomplishment when players overcome them. In this chapter, we will dive into how to design and implement obstacles, create hazards, and design AI (Artificial Intelligence) for enemies that behave in various ways to challenge the player.

Placing Obstacles and Creating Hazards

Obstacles and hazards are the elements that players need to avoid, overcome, or interact with as they progress through the game. These elements are critical for creating tension, excitement, and pacing within your levels.

1. **Types of Obstacles and Hazards**:
    - **Environmental Obstacles**: These could include pits, spikes, boulders, or falling platforms. These obstacles require the player to time their jumps, movements, or decisions carefully.

        - *Example*: Spikes that cause damage if touched or moving platforms that the player must jump across to avoid falling.
    - **Hazardous Zones**: These could include toxic sludge, fire pits, or lava. Stepping into these areas could damage or kill the player, creating a risk for exploration.
        - *Example*: A pool of acid that deals damage over time as the player stands in it, encouraging quick decision-making.

2. **Placing Obstacles**:
    - **Spacing and Difficulty**: When placing obstacles, think about how they affect the flow of gameplay. Don't overload your level with too many obstacles in a small area. Gradually increase the difficulty by placing obstacles in more challenging spots as the player progresses.
    - **Creating Patterns**: In platformer games, obstacles often follow patterns that players must learn to navigate. You can create a rhythm of moving platforms or enemies to test the player's reaction time and strategic thinking.
    - **Challenge vs. Frustration**: While it's important to make obstacles challenging, it's also crucial to avoid frustrating the player. Make sure there's

always a way to overcome an obstacle and that the player isn't punished unfairly for mistakes.

3. **Implementing Obstacles in Unity**:
   - Use Unity's **colliders** to create the hitboxes for obstacles. For stationary obstacles, a simple **BoxCollider2D** or **CircleCollider2D** will suffice.
   - For moving obstacles, you can use Unity's **Rigidbody2D** to apply physics, or use scripts to control their movement patterns.
   - For hazards like fire or spikes, attach **trigger colliders** to detect when the player comes into contact with the hazard, and apply damage or other effects accordingly.

Designing AI for Basic Enemies

Enemies are an integral part of many games, and their behavior is often what provides players with the most challenge. Basic enemy AI in 2D games often involves detecting the player's presence and responding by moving toward, avoiding, or patrolling certain areas.

1. **Types of Enemy Behavior**:

- **Static Enemies**: These enemies stay in one place, often guarding specific areas or acting as obstacles that the player must avoid.
- **Patrolling Enemies**: These enemies follow a set path, often moving back and forth between two points. Their behavior is simple, and the challenge for the player comes from timing their movements to avoid being detected or caught.
- **Chasing Enemies**: These enemies actively follow the player, typically when the player is within a certain range. The challenge here is evading them or finding ways to outsmart them.
- **Flying or Jumping Enemies**: Some enemies can move in the air, creating additional layers of difficulty. These enemies can chase or patrol along vertical paths and often require the player to engage with them in different ways.

2. **Basic Enemy AI in Unity**: Unity provides a variety of ways to implement enemy behavior. A basic AI system can be created using simple scripts and Unity's physics system. Here's how you can begin:
   - **Movement and Navigation**:
     - For patrolling, you can use waypoints. Create empty GameObjects in the scene that mark the points where an enemy

should move to. Use a script to move the enemy between these points.

- For chasing, you can use Unity's **Vector2.Distance** method to calculate the distance between the enemy and the player. If the player is within a certain range, the enemy will follow the player.

Example:

```
csharp
CopyEdit
void Update() {
    float      distanceToPlayer      =
Vector2.Distance(transform.position
, player.position);
    if      (distanceToPlayer      <
chaseRange) {
        // Move towards player
        Vector2      direction      =
(player.position                    -
transform.position).normalized;

transform.Translate(direction       *
speed * Time.deltaTime);
    }
}
```

- **Animation**: You can add animations to your enemies to show different states like idle, patrolling, or attacking. Use Unity's **Animator** component to handle transitions between these animations based on the enemy's behavior.
- **Detection**: To detect the player, you can use simple distance checks or Unity's **Raycast** to check if there is a clear line of sight between the enemy and the player. You can then adjust the enemy's behavior accordingly (e.g., switch to chasing mode if the player is detected).

Creating Different Behaviors (e.g., Moving, Chasing, Patrolling)

Once you have a basic understanding of how to implement enemy movement, it's time to expand and create more sophisticated behaviors for your enemies.

1. **Patrolling Behavior**:
    - Patrolling is one of the most common enemy behaviors. Enemies that patrol a specific area create a rhythm that players must learn and react to.
    - You can define patrol points using empty GameObjects as waypoints, and use a script to move the enemy back and forth between them.

Example:

```
csharp
CopyEdit
public Transform[] patrolPoints;
private int currentPoint = 0;

void Update() {
    Transform targetPoint =
patrolPoints[currentPoint];
    transform.position =
Vector2.MoveTowards(transform.position,
targetPoint.position, speed *
Time.deltaTime);

    if
(Vector2.Distance(transform.position,
targetPoint.position) < 0.2f) {
        currentPoint = (currentPoint + 1)
% patrolPoints.Length;
    }
}
```

2. **Chasing Behavior**:
    - Chasing enemies actively pursue the player once they come within a certain range. The simplest way to implement this is by checking the distance between the enemy and the player and moving the

enemy toward the player's position when they are close enough.

Example:

```
csharp
CopyEdit
void Update() {
    if
(Vector2.Distance(transform.position,
player.position) < chaseRange) {
        Vector2         direction         =
(player.position                          -
transform.position).normalized;
        transform.position                =
Vector2.MoveTowards(transform.position,
player.position,        chaseSpeed        *
Time.deltaTime);
    }
}
```

3. **Avoiding Obstacles**:
    - Enemies may need to avoid obstacles while chasing the player. Implementing **Raycasting** allows enemies to detect walls or other objects in front of them and steer around them. This makes AI more dynamic and creates a more challenging environment for players.

- Using **NavMesh** or **pathfinding algorithms** is another approach, especially if you're building more complex AI for large areas.

Summary

In this chapter, we've explored how to introduce obstacles and enemies into your game, both of which are key to creating a challenging and engaging experience. By strategically placing obstacles and hazards, you can control the pacing and difficulty of your levels, making them more enjoyable to navigate.

We also dove into enemy AI, covering basic behaviors like patrolling, chasing, and moving. With Unity's powerful tools, you can quickly design enemies with simple scripts that respond to the player's actions. By experimenting with different AI behaviors, you can create dynamic and unpredictable challenges that will keep players on their toes.

With these concepts in hand, you are now equipped to populate your game world with a variety of obstacles and enemies, enriching the player's experience with dynamic interactions and challenges.

CHAPTER 10

IMPLEMENTING GAME UI

A well-designed user interface (UI) is crucial to a player's overall experience, providing them with important information and a way to interact with the game. In this chapter, we'll dive into the essentials of implementing a simple UI in Unity, covering topics such as creating a heads-up display (HUD) for health, score, and other vital stats, as well as handling menus, pause screens, and button interactions.

Designing and Implementing a Simple HUD (Health, Score, etc.)

The HUD is the primary way players interact with your game while playing. It provides crucial information, such as health, score, time, and other relevant statistics, without interrupting the gameplay.

1. **Setting Up the HUD**: Unity makes it easy to create a HUD using its **UI system**. The UI elements are placed in a **Canvas** component, which is responsible for rendering UI elements on the screen. You can access the Canvas from the Unity Editor by right-clicking in the **Hierarchy** window and selecting **UI** > **Canvas**.

2. **Health Display**: A health bar is a common element in many games, providing the player with real-time feedback on their character's health. You can represent the health bar using a **Slider** or **Image** component.
   - **Using a Slider for Health**:
     - Right-click in the **Hierarchy** > **UI** > **Slider** to create a new slider.
     - Set the **Min Value** to 0 (for no health) and the **Max Value** to the character's maximum health.
     - To update the health bar during gameplay, you can script it to change the **Slider's value** as the player's health decreases or increases.

   Example code:

```
csharp
CopyEdit
public Slider healthSlider;
public float maxHealth = 100f;
public float currentHealth = 100f;

void Update() {
    healthSlider.value =
currentHealth / maxHealth;
}
```

- **Using an Image for Health**: Alternatively, you can use an **Image** element with a fill method to display the health bar as a filling progress bar.
  - Right-click in the **Hierarchy** > **UI** > **Image**.
  - Set the **Fill Method** to **Horizontal** and adjust the **Fill Amount** in the script.

3. **Score Display**: A score is typically displayed as a simple text element. To implement this, use the **Text** UI element:
   - Right-click in the **Hierarchy** > **UI** > **Text** to create a new text field.
   - Place it in a suitable spot on the screen (typically at the top-left or top-right corner).
   - In your script, update the score and reflect it on the UI as the player earns points.

   Example code:

```
csharp
CopyEdit
public Text scoreText;
public int score = 0;

void Update() {
    scoreText.text = "Score: " +
score;
}
```

4. **Other HUD Elements**: You can add additional information to the HUD, such as:
    - **Timer**: If your game has a time limit, a timer can be displayed using a **Text** element.
    - **Ammo**: Display remaining ammo or power-ups with icons or text.
    - **Level Progress**: Show progress through a level or current objectives.

Handling Menus, Pause Screens, and Transitions

Menus and pause screens are integral parts of most games, allowing players to pause the game, adjust settings, or navigate between different scenes.

1. **Creating Menus**: Menus are usually simple screens with buttons that allow the player to interact with the game. Common menus include:
    - **Main Menu**: Presented at the start of the game, with options to start the game, access settings, or quit.
    - **Game Over Screen**: Displayed when the player loses, often showing their score and options to retry or return to the main menu.

To create a menu, add **UI Text**, **Buttons**, and other elements to the **Canvas**. For example, a main menu might have a "Start Game" button, a "Settings" button, and a "Quit" button.

2. **Creating a Pause Screen**: The pause screen pauses the game and typically gives the player the option to resume or quit. To implement a pause screen:
    - Create a new **Canvas** that contains a panel for the pause screen. This panel will be shown or hidden based on whether the game is paused.
    - Use a button to resume the game, and another to quit or go to the main menu.
    - You can control the game's pause state by toggling the **Time.timeScale**.

    Example code to pause the game:

    ```
    csharp
    CopyEdit
    public GameObject pausePanel;

    void Update() {
        if
    (Input.GetKeyDown(KeyCode.Escape)) {
            TogglePause();
        }
    }
    ```

```
void TogglePause() {
    bool  isPaused  =  Time.timeScale
== 0;
    Time.timeScale = isPaused ? 1 :
0;  // Resume or pause the game

pausePanel.SetActive(!isPaused);
// Show or hide the pause panel
}
```

3. **Scene Transitions**: Menus and screens often require transitioning between different scenes (e.g., from the main menu to the game scene, or from the game to the game over screen). You can handle scene transitions using Unity's **SceneManager**.
   - To load a scene, use the following code:

```
csharp
CopyEdit
using UnityEngine.SceneManagement;

public     void     LoadScene(string
sceneName) {

SceneManager.LoadScene(sceneName);
}
```

- You can call this method when a button is clicked in the UI (e.g., when the player presses the "Start Game" button, the game scene is loaded).

Creating Buttons and User Interactions

Buttons are the primary method for interacting with the UI in many games. You can create buttons for actions such as starting the game, restarting, or quitting.

1. **Creating Buttons**:
   - Right-click in the **Hierarchy** > **UI** > **Button** to create a new button.
   - In the **Inspector** window, you can customize the button's **Text** and appearance by changing its **Image** or **Text** components.
   - To assign an action to the button (e.g., to start the game), you will need to link a function to the button's **OnClick** event.
2. **Assigning Functions to Buttons**:
   - In the **Button** component, find the **OnClick()** event. You can add a function from any script to this event. For example, if you have a function in your script called `StartGame`, you can assign this function to the button click.

Example:

```
csharp
CopyEdit
public void StartGame() {

SceneManager.LoadScene("GameScene")
;
}
```

3. **Button Interaction Feedback**:
   - Unity provides built-in interaction feedback for buttons, such as **Hover**, **Pressed**, and **Selected** states. You can customize these using the **Button** component's **Transition** property, choosing from color changes, animations, or sounds.
   - For example, you can change the button color when the player hovers over it. Unity allows you to do this through the **Color Tint** option in the Button's **Transition** settings.

Summary

In this chapter, we've covered the essential aspects of implementing a user interface (UI) in Unity, including designing a simple HUD for displaying vital information like health and score. We also learned how to handle menus, pause screens, and scene transitions, which are critical for improving the player experience by providing smooth navigation between different parts of the game. Finally, we explored how to create buttons and other interactive UI elements to allow the player to control the game and interact with its features.

By mastering these UI techniques, you can create a professional and intuitive interface for your game, giving players the tools they need to navigate and interact with your game world seamlessly.

CHAPTER 11

SOUND DESIGN AND MUSIC

Sound plays a vital role in immersing players and enhancing the overall experience of a game. Whether it's the sound of a character jumping, the background music, or the eerie noises in a dark dungeon, audio helps bring the game world to life. In this chapter, we will explore how to implement sound effects, loop background music, trigger sounds based on in-game events, and adjust audio for different devices.

Importing and Using Sound Effects

Sound effects are integral to creating feedback for player actions and events in your game. Whether it's a character jumping, an explosion, or a power-up being collected, sound effects add realism and depth to your game world.

1. **Importing Audio Files**: Unity supports a variety of audio file formats, including **WAV**, **MP3**, **OGG**, and **AIFF**. To import a sound effect:
    - Simply drag and drop the audio file into the **Assets** folder in Unity's **Project** window.

   - Unity automatically imports the sound and creates an **AudioClip** asset.
2. **Using Audio Clips**: To use a sound effect in your game, create an **AudioSource** component:
   - Right-click in the **Hierarchy** window > **Create Empty** to create a new GameObject.
   - With the GameObject selected, in the **Inspector**, click **Add Component** and choose **AudioSource**.
   - In the **AudioSource** component, drag and drop the desired AudioClip into the **AudioClip** field.
   - To play the sound, use the following C# code in your script:

```
csharp
CopyEdit
public AudioSource audioSource;

void PlaySound() {
    audioSource.Play();
}
```

3. **Playing Sounds at Specific Points**:
   - To trigger sound effects based on in-game events (e.g., when the player collects a coin or shoots a weapon), call the **Play()** method of the **AudioSource** when the event occurs.

Example:

```
csharp
CopyEdit
public AudioClip collectSound;
private AudioSource audioSource;

void Start() {
    audioSource                                    =
GetComponent<AudioSource>();
}

void OnTriggerEnter2D(Collider2D other) {
    if (other.CompareTag("Coin")) {

audioSource.PlayOneShot(collectSound);   //
Play the sound once
    }
}
```

- The **PlayOneShot()** method is useful for playing a sound effect only once at a given point, without interrupting any currently playing sounds.

Looping Background Music and Sound Triggers

Background music sets the tone of the game and helps immerse players into the environment. Additionally, sound triggers are crucial for events that occur periodically or in response to player actions.

1. **Looping Background Music**: To add background music that loops throughout the game, follow these steps:
    - Import your music file as described above.
    - Create a new **AudioSource** component on a GameObject (e.g., your **Main Camera** or a dedicated **AudioManager**).
    - Assign the music file to the **AudioClip** property of the AudioSource.
    - Set the **Loop** property of the AudioSource to **true** to make it loop indefinitely during gameplay.

    Example:

```
csharp
CopyEdit
public AudioClip backgroundMusic;
private AudioSource audioSource;

void Start() {
    audioSource                                    =
GetComponent<AudioSource>();
    audioSource.clip = backgroundMusic;
    audioSource.loop = true;   // Set the
music to loop
    audioSource.Play();          // Start
playing the music
```

```
}
```

2. **Triggering Sounds Based on Events**: Sound effects can be triggered by in-game events, such as a character's death, an enemy attack, or a level transition.

   Example:

```
csharp
CopyEdit
public AudioClip explosionSound;
private AudioSource audioSource;

void Start() {
    audioSource                                    =
GetComponent<AudioSource>();
}

void Explode() {
    // Trigger explosion sound when the
event occurs

audioSource.PlayOneShot(explosionSound);
}
```

   This method ensures that specific sound effects are played at the right time, adding to the game's dynamic atmosphere.

3. **Spatial Sound**: To create a more immersive sound experience, you can use spatial sound, which allows sounds to vary based on their position relative to the player. This is especially important in 3D games but can also enhance 2D games with a "panning" effect.
   - Enable **3D Sound** by setting the **Spatial Blend** property of the AudioSource to 1 (fully 3D).
   - Adjust the **Min Distance** and **Max Distance** to control how sound fades as the player moves away from the sound source.

   Example:

```
csharp
CopyEdit
audioSource.spatialBlend = 1.0f;   // Full 3D sound
audioSource.minDistance = 5.0f;    // Sound is heard clearly within 5 units
audioSource.maxDistance = 20.0f;   // Sound starts to fade after 20 units
```

Adjusting Audio for Different Devices (Volume, Pitch, etc.)

Different devices (PCs, mobile phones, consoles) often have varying audio output capabilities, so it's important to ensure that your game's audio is well-adjusted for each device.

1. **Adjusting Volume**: Unity's **AudioListener** allows you to control global audio volume. You can adjust the master volume or individual volume levels using sliders or in-game settings.
   - To adjust the volume of an **AudioSource** directly, use the `volume` property:

     ```
     csharp
     CopyEdit
     audioSource.volume = 0.5f;   // Set
     the volume to 50%
     ```

   - For global volume control, you can adjust the **AudioListener.volume**:

     ```
     csharp
     CopyEdit
     AudioListener.volume = 0.5f;  // Set
     global volume to 50%
     ```

2. **Adjusting Pitch**: To make the sound higher or lower in pitch, modify the **pitch** property of the **AudioSource**.
   - A pitch of 1 is the normal pitch, values above 1 increase the pitch, and values below 1 decrease the pitch.

Example:

```
csharp
```

```
CopyEdit
audioSource.pitch = 1.2f;  // Increase the
pitch by 20%
```

Adjusting pitch is useful for creating variations in sound effects. For example, you might want to change the pitch of a jump sound based on the player's speed or actions.

3. **Handling Device-Specific Audio**: Audio output on different platforms might require adjustments in terms of volume, stereo balance, and spatial effects. For mobile devices, it's important to provide an in-game audio settings menu that allows players to adjust the sound quality to match their device's capabilities.

   Unity also provides the **AudioSettings** API for advanced configurations, allowing you to set sample rates or quality settings based on the target device.

   Example:

   ```
   csharp
   CopyEdit
   AudioSettings.outputSampleRate = 44100;
   // Set the output sample rate for better
   quality
   ```

4. **Supporting Different Audio Systems**: On mobile devices, you might need to adjust the audio settings for

mono or stereo output depending on the device's speakers or headphones. For instance, on mono devices, you may want to force the audio to play through both speakers equally.

Summary

In this chapter, we've explored the essentials of sound design and music implementation in Unity. Sound effects and music are key components that contribute to the emotional atmosphere and gameplay experience. You've learned how to import and use sound effects, create looping background music, and trigger sound events based on in-game actions.

We also covered how to adjust audio for different devices, ensuring that your game sounds great on a variety of platforms. With spatial sound features, pitch and volume adjustments, and platform-specific audio settings, you can ensure that your game delivers a rich and immersive sound experience for all players.

By implementing these sound features, you'll be able to craft a more engaging and polished experience for players, adding depth to the world you've created and helping them connect with the game on a deeper level.

CHAPTER 12

ANIMATION AND VISUAL EFFECTS

Animations and visual effects (VFX) are crucial for making a game dynamic and engaging. They help breathe life into the game world, providing players with visual feedback on their actions and enhancing the overall aesthetic. In this chapter, we'll explore how to create and implement animations in Unity, work with particle effects, and transition between animations based on the game state.

Creating Animations Using Unity's Animator

Unity's **Animator** system provides a powerful toolset for creating and controlling animations within your game. Whether it's a simple character walk cycle or complex character actions, the Animator allows you to design, manage, and transition between different animations.

1. **Setting Up the Animator**: To start animating in Unity:
    - Create a **GameObject** (for example, your player character).

- Add an **Animator** component to the GameObject by selecting the object in the **Hierarchy** window and clicking **Add Component** > **Animator**.
- In the **Animator** window, Unity will display the Animator Controller. If one is not automatically created, you can create one by right-clicking in the **Project** window > **Create** > **Animator Controller**.

2. **Creating Animations**: You can create animations directly in Unity by recording keyframes for specific properties (e.g., position, rotation, scale, or sprite changes for 2D sprites).
   - **For 2D Sprites**: Right-click in the **Assets** window and choose **Create** > **Animation** to create a new animation. Unity will then open the **Animation** window.
   - To animate a 2D sprite, select the object to be animated, click **Add Property**, and select the property (like **Sprite Renderer > Sprite**) you want to animate. Then, use the timeline to set keyframes at specific points in time, adjusting the sprite or other properties.
   - **For 3D Models**: The process is similar but with 3D meshes. You can animate movement, rotation, scale, or any other mesh-related property.

3. **Creating Animation Clips**: An animation clip contains the keyframes for an animation. Each animation clip can be linked to a specific action (e.g., walking, jumping, or shooting).

   To create an animation:

   - Select the **Animation** window and hit **Record** to start creating keyframes.
   - Move the playhead to different time points and change the property (e.g., position or sprite), and Unity will automatically add keyframes.
   - You can adjust the **Speed** of the animation to control how fast or slow it plays.

4. **Adding Transitions Between Animations**: Once you have multiple animations (e.g., idle, run, jump), you can set up transitions between them.
   - In the **Animator** window, you can create a **State Machine**, where each state represents an animation clip.
   - **Transitions** are created by right-clicking on a state and selecting **Make Transition**. Then, you drag the arrow to the destination state.
   - You can control when transitions happen by defining **Conditions**. For example, when the player presses the jump button, transition from the "Idle" animation to the "Jump" animation.

Implementing Particle Effects (e.g., Explosions, Sparks)

Particle effects are often used for creating dynamic visual effects like explosions, fire, sparks, smoke, and magic. Unity's **Particle System** is a versatile tool for creating such effects. Here's how to set up and use particle effects in Unity:

1. **Creating a Particle System**:
    - To create a particle system, right-click in the **Hierarchy** > **Effects** > **Particle System**. This will create a new particle system GameObject.
    - The Particle System component will have default settings, including a basic effect that emits particles over time.
2. **Customizing the Particle System**: The **Particle System** has many settings that allow you to control various aspects of the effect:
    - **Duration**: The time the particle system will emit particles before stopping.
    - **Start Lifetime**: How long each particle lasts before disappearing.
    - **Start Size**: The size of each particle.
    - **Start Speed**: The speed at which the particles move.
    - **Start Color**: The color of the particles.

- **Emitter Shape**: Determines the shape from which particles are emitted (e.g., sphere, cone, box, etc.).

You can adjust these properties to create effects like sparks, smoke, explosions, and more.

3. **Creating Explosions and Sparks**: For an explosion effect, you might want to emit a large number of particles with a short lifetime, with a high initial speed, and a burst shape:
   - Set the **Shape** to **Sphere** to create an explosion effect.
   - Increase the **Start Size** and **Start Speed** to make the particles appear larger and move faster.
   - Set the **Start Color** to something like **yellow, orange**, and **red** to simulate fire and explosions.

Example of an explosion:

```
csharp
CopyEdit
public ParticleSystem explosionEffect;

void Explode() {
    explosionEffect.Play();   // Play the
explosion particle effect
}
```

You can trigger this effect when an explosion occurs in your game (e.g., when an enemy is destroyed).

4. **Handling Multiple Particle Systems**: For complex effects (such as smoke trails or fire), you might use multiple particle systems working together. For example, a fire effect may consist of one particle system for the flames and another for smoke.

   To handle multiple particle systems, you can attach them to the same GameObject or use child GameObjects for each effect, making it easy to control and trigger them individually.

Transitioning Between Animations Based on Game State

In Unity, transitioning between animations based on the game state (e.g., idle, walking, jumping, attacking) is crucial for smooth gameplay. You can use the Animator's **Parameters** and **Transitions** to handle these dynamic changes.

1. **Setting Up Parameters**: To control when transitions occur, you can create **parameters** in the Animator. These parameters can be of various types:
   - **Trigger**: Used to activate a specific animation (e.g., an attack animation when a button is pressed).

- **Bool**: Used for binary conditions (e.g., whether the player is grounded or not).
- **Float**: Used for continuous values (e.g., player speed).
- **Int**: Used for integer values.

Example: Create a **float** parameter for player speed and a **bool** parameter for whether the player is jumping.

- **Speed** (float): Controls how fast the character moves.
- **IsJumping** (bool): Whether the character is in the air.

2. **Changing Parameters via Script**: In your game script, you can modify the parameters based on game events. For instance, when the player starts walking, you set the **Speed** parameter, and when they jump, you toggle the **IsJumping** parameter.

Example code:

```
csharp
CopyEdit
public Animator animator;

void Update() {
```

```
    float speed = Mathf.Abs(horizontalInput);    // Get the player's speed
    animator.SetFloat("Speed", speed);  // Update the Speed parameter in Animator

    if (isJumping) {
        animator.SetBool("IsJumping", true);  // Set jumping state
    } else {
        animator.SetBool("IsJumping", false);  // Set idle or running state
    }
}
```

3. **Animator Transitions**: In the **Animator** window, you can set conditions for transitioning between animations. For example:
   - When **Speed** > 0, transition from the "Idle" animation to the "Run" animation.
   - When **IsJumping** is true, transition to the "Jump" animation.

   Unity automatically blends animations based on these conditions, allowing for smooth transitions between different states.

4. **Animation Transitions with Time**: You can control how quickly the animation switches from one to another using

the **Transition Duration**. A shorter duration results in quicker transitions, while a longer duration creates a smoother, more gradual change.

  - You can also set **Exit Time** to define when the animation should end before transitioning (e.g., finishing the jump animation before transitioning to idle).

Summary

In this chapter, we've explored how to create and implement animations and visual effects in Unity to enhance your game's experience. You've learned how to set up animations using Unity's **Animator**, how to create particle effects such as explosions and sparks, and how to manage transitions between animations based on game states.

By mastering animation and visual effects, you can significantly improve the feel of your game, making it more immersive and responsive to player actions. Whether it's for a smooth walking animation or a dramatic explosion effect, animations and VFX add that extra layer of polish that turns a simple game into a memorable experience.

CHAPTER 13

MANAGING GAME OBJECTS AND SCENES

In game development, the way you organize and manage your game objects and scenes is crucial for keeping your project efficient and scalable. This chapter will cover the fundamentals of Unity's **GameObjects** and **Prefabs**, introduce you to **scene management**, and explain how to use multiple scenes effectively in a game. By understanding these concepts, you'll be able to structure your game in a way that's both modular and easy to manage, even as it grows.

Understanding GameObjects and Prefabs

Unity's **GameObjects** are the basic building blocks of any game. Every object in your game, whether it's a character, an item, or an environmental object, is represented by a GameObject.

1. **GameObjects**:
    - A **GameObject** is an empty container that can hold components (e.g., renderers, colliders, scripts) which define its appearance and behavior.

- In Unity, you can create a new GameObject by right-clicking in the **Hierarchy** window and selecting the appropriate type (e.g., **2D Object** for sprites or **3D Object** for meshes).
- GameObjects don't do anything on their own. They require components to provide functionality. For instance, a **Sprite Renderer** component will make a GameObject visible as a 2D sprite, and a **Rigidbody2D** will add physics interactions.

Example:

```
csharp
CopyEdit
public GameObject player;  // A reference
to the player GameObject

void Start() {
    player   =   GameObject.Find("Player");
// Find and assign the player GameObject at
runtime
}
```

2. **Prefabs**:
   - A **Prefab** is a reusable GameObject template that you can create from a GameObject in the

Hierarchy window by dragging it into the **Project** window.

- Prefabs are a powerful feature in Unity because they allow you to instantiate copies of the same object in multiple places. If you make a change to a prefab, all instances of that prefab will automatically update.
- Prefabs are ideal for creating objects that appear in multiple places in your game (like enemies, obstacles, or interactive items), ensuring consistency and reducing the need for repetitive work.

To create a prefab:

- Select a GameObject in the **Hierarchy** window.
- Drag it into the **Project** window.

Example of instantiating a prefab at runtime:

```
csharp
CopyEdit
public GameObject enemyPrefab;

void SpawnEnemy(Vector3 position) {
    Instantiate(enemyPrefab,     position,
Quaternion.identity);   // Instantiate the
prefab at a given position
```

```
}
```

Scene Transitions and Management

Scenes in Unity are containers for all the GameObjects that make up your game's environment. A typical game will consist of multiple scenes, such as a main menu, different levels, and a game over screen. Managing these scenes and transitioning between them is a key skill for building functional games.

1. **Scene Management**: Unity's **Scene Management** system allows you to load, unload, and transition between different scenes. You can use the built-in **SceneManager** class to manage these transitions.
   - **Loading and Unloading Scenes**: You can load and unload scenes either synchronously or asynchronously.
   - **Async Loading**: Asynchronous loading allows you to load scenes in the background while keeping the game running smoothly. This is especially useful for large scenes or when you want to maintain game performance during loading screens.

Example of loading a scene:

```
csharp
```

```
CopyEdit
using UnityEngine.SceneManagement;

void LoadNextLevel() {
    SceneManager.LoadScene("Level2");    //
Load the scene named "Level2"
}
```

2. **Scene Transitions**:
   - Scene transitions are the moments when the game changes from one scene to another. Unity's SceneManager provides several ways to handle these transitions.
   - You can use **SceneManager.LoadScene()** to load a new scene when certain events happen, such as completing a level or clicking a button on the menu.

Example of transitioning to a new scene with a fade effect:

```
csharp
CopyEdit
using UnityEngine.SceneManagement;

public Animator transitionAnimator;

void StartGame() {
```

```
transitionAnimator.SetTrigger("FadeOut");
// Trigger fade-out animation
    Invoke("LoadScene", 1f);   // Wait for
fade-out to complete before loading the
scene
}

void LoadScene() {
    SceneManager.LoadScene("GameLevel1");
// Load the new scene
}
```

Using Multiple Scenes in a Game (e.g., Main Menu, Levels)

A game typically consists of more than one scene. For instance, you may have a **Main Menu**, various **Levels**, and a **Game Over** screen. Unity provides powerful tools for managing these scenes and ensuring that your game runs smoothly as it transitions from one to the next.

1. **Multiple Scene Setup**:
   - In Unity, you can have multiple scenes open at once (though only one is active). For example, you could have a **Game Level** scene and a **UI** scene (such as the Main Menu) running simultaneously.

   - To manage multiple scenes, use the **SceneManager.LoadScene** function or **SceneManager.LoadSceneAsync** to load a new scene when needed.

Example of using the **Additive** mode to load multiple scenes:

```
csharp
CopyEdit
SceneManager.LoadScene("MainMenu",
LoadSceneMode.Additive);  // Load MainMenu
without unloading the current scene
```

2. **Main Menu Scene**:
   - The **Main Menu** is typically the first scene that loads when the game starts. It contains buttons for starting the game, adjusting settings, or quitting.
   - To load the game from the main menu, you might transition to the first level, triggering a scene change with a button press.

Example of loading a level from the main menu:

```
csharp
CopyEdit
public void OnStartButtonClicked() {
```

```
    SceneManager.LoadScene("Level1");    //
Load the first level when the start button
is clicked
}
```

3. **Level Transitions**:
   - Levels in a game are usually separated into different scenes, making it easier to organize your project and load smaller pieces of content when needed.
   - Transitions between levels can be enhanced by using animation effects, loading screens, or fade-in/out effects to mask the loading process.

Example of transitioning to the next level with a fade effect:

```
csharp
CopyEdit
public Animator transitionAnimator;

void LoadNextLevel() {

transitionAnimator.SetTrigger("FadeOut");
// Trigger the fade-out animation
    Invoke("NextLevel", 1f);  // Delay the
scene change until the animation finishes
}
```

```
void NextLevel() {
    SceneManager.LoadScene("NextLevel");
// Load the next level
}
```

4. **Game Over and Restart**:
   - When the player loses, you can transition to a **Game Over** scene, which might show a score, options to restart, or quit the game.
   - Similarly, a **Restart** button on the game over screen can reload the current level or reset the game.

Example of restarting the level:

```
csharp
CopyEdit
public void RestartLevel() {

SceneManager.LoadScene(SceneManager.GetAc
tiveScene().name);  // Reload the current
level
}
```

Summary

In this chapter, we've explored the essentials of managing **GameObjects** and **Prefabs** in Unity, and how to effectively handle **scene transitions** and multiple scenes. By understanding the relationship between GameObjects and Prefabs, you can create reusable and easily configurable assets. Furthermore, mastering scene management allows you to efficiently organize and navigate between different parts of your game, such as menus, levels, and game over screens.

Managing GameObjects and scenes effectively is key to maintaining an organized project, especially as your game grows in complexity. With this knowledge, you're well-equipped to build games that are scalable, modular, and provide smooth transitions between various game states.

CHAPTER 14

ADDING SCORING AND PROGRESSION

A key element in most games is the ability to track player progress and provide feedback on performance. This chapter will cover how to implement a **scoring system**, manage **player progression**, including level-ups and power-ups, and introduce the concept of **saving game progress** using Unity's **PlayerPrefs** system. By the end of this chapter, you'll be able to add dynamic and rewarding systems to your game, enhancing the player experience.

Implementing a Scoring System

A **scoring system** allows you to track and display a player's performance in the game. Whether it's points earned by collecting items, defeating enemies, or completing levels, a score provides immediate feedback to the player. Here's how you can create and manage a basic scoring system in Unity.

1. **Basic Score System**:
   - You can store the score using a simple integer variable.

- When certain actions happen in the game (e.g., the player defeats an enemy or completes a level), you can increase or decrease the score accordingly.

Example:

```
csharp
CopyEdit
public int score = 0;  // Player's score

void AddScore(int points) {
    score += points;   // Add points to
score
    UpdateScoreDisplay();   // Update the
score on the UI
}

void UpdateScoreDisplay() {
    scoreText.text   =   "Score:   "   +
score.ToString();  // Display the score on
the UI
}
```

2. **Displaying the Score**:
   - To show the score in the game, you will need to create a **UI Text** element in Unity and update it each time the score changes.

- Use Unity's **Text** component (or **TextMeshPro** for better text rendering) to display the current score.

Example:

```
csharp
CopyEdit
public Text scoreText;  // Reference to the
UI Text component

void Start() {
    scoreText                                    =
GameObject.Find("ScoreText").GetComponent
<Text>();  // Find the Text object
}
```

3. **Increasing the Score**:
   - You can increase the score when the player defeats an enemy or collects a collectible item.

Example (collecting an item):

```
csharp
CopyEdit
void OnTriggerEnter2D(Collider2D other) {
    if (other.CompareTag("Collectible")) {
        AddScore(10);    // Add 10 points
when the player collects an item
```

```
        Destroy(other.gameObject);        //
Destroy the collectible item
    }
}
```

Player Progression (Level-Ups, Power-Ups)

In many games, players earn rewards or power-ups that help them progress through the game. **Level-ups** and **power-ups** are common mechanics that provide players with a sense of achievement and a reason to keep playing.

1. **Level-Ups**:
    - Players often level up after reaching a certain amount of experience or points. When a player levels up, they could gain new abilities, stronger stats, or unlock new content.

Example:

```
csharp
CopyEdit
public int playerLevel = 1;
public int experiencePoints = 0;
public int experienceThreshold = 100;   //
Experience required for leveling up

void GainExperience(int points) {
```

```
    experiencePoints += points;
    if          (experiencePoints          >=
experienceThreshold) {
        LevelUp();
    }
}

void LevelUp() {
    playerLevel++;
    experiencePoints   =   0;     //   Reset
experience
    experienceThreshold += 50;  // Increase
threshold for next level
    UpdateLevelDisplay();   // Update  the
level on the UI
}

void UpdateLevelDisplay() {
    levelText.text    =    "Level:    "    +
playerLevel.ToString();   //  Display  the
level on the UI
}
```

2. **Power-Ups**:
   - Power-ups give players temporary boosts, such as increased speed, invincibility, or double damage. These are often collected as items in the game world.

Example:

```
csharp
CopyEdit
public bool isInvincible = false;
public float invincibilityDuration = 5f;

void OnTriggerEnter2D(Collider2D other) {
    if (other.CompareTag("PowerUp")) {
        ActivatePowerUp();
        Destroy(other.gameObject);        //
Destroy the power-up item
    }
}

void ActivatePowerUp() {
    isInvincible = true;
    Invoke("DeactivatePowerUp",
invincibilityDuration);     //  Deactivate
after duration
}

void DeactivatePowerUp() {
    isInvincible = false;
}
```

In this example, the player gains invincibility for a limited time upon collecting the power-up.

Saving Game Progress with PlayerPrefs

To provide a more personalized and persistent experience, you may want to save the player's progress between sessions. Unity provides a built-in system called **PlayerPrefs** for storing and retrieving simple data like scores, levels, or settings. **PlayerPrefs** allows you to save and load data easily without needing complex databases or external files.

1. **Saving Player Progress**:
   - You can use **PlayerPrefs.SetInt()**, **PlayerPrefs.SetFloat()**, or **PlayerPrefs.SetString()** to save the player's progress, such as score or level.
   - For instance, to save the player's score:

Example:

```
csharp
CopyEdit
public void SaveProgress() {
    PlayerPrefs.SetInt("Score",    score);
// Save score
    PlayerPrefs.SetInt("PlayerLevel",
playerLevel);  // Save player level
    PlayerPrefs.Save();   // Make sure to
save the data
}
```

2. **Loading Player Progress**:
   - To load the saved data, use **PlayerPrefs.GetInt()**, **PlayerPrefs.GetFloat()**, or **PlayerPrefs.GetString()**. If the key doesn't exist, you can provide a default value.

Example:

```
csharp
CopyEdit
public void LoadProgress() {
    score = PlayerPrefs.GetInt("Score", 0);  // Load score, default to 0 if not found
    playerLevel = PlayerPrefs.GetInt("PlayerLevel", 1);  // Load player level, default to 1 if not found
    UpdateScoreDisplay();  // Update the score UI
    UpdateLevelDisplay();  // Update the level UI
}
```

3. **Clearing Saved Progress**:
   - If you want to reset the player's progress, use **PlayerPrefs.DeleteKey()** or **PlayerPrefs.DeleteAll()** to delete specific keys or all saved data.

Example:

```
csharp
CopyEdit
public void ResetProgress() {
    PlayerPrefs.DeleteAll();    //  Delete
all saved progress
}
```

Summary

In this chapter, we've covered how to create a **scoring system**, implement **player progression** (including level-ups and power-ups), and use **PlayerPrefs** to save and load game progress. A well-designed scoring and progression system enhances player engagement by providing feedback and rewards for achievements. Saving game progress allows players to pick up right where they left off, ensuring a seamless and enjoyable experience across multiple sessions. With these tools at your disposal, you can create a dynamic and persistent game world that motivates players to keep playing.

CHAPTER 15

GAME CAMERA AND VIEWPORT MANAGEMENT

In any game, the camera serves as the player's window into the world, dictating what they can see and how they interact with the environment. In 2D games, the camera plays an even more significant role because it directly affects how players experience the game world. This chapter will guide you through setting up and managing the camera in Unity, making it follow the player, and adding dynamic camera effects like shake and zoom to enhance gameplay.

Setting Up and Managing the Camera in 2D Games

Unity provides a built-in **Camera** component, which allows you to control how the game world is rendered on the screen. When developing 2D games, you need to set up the camera to give players the best possible view of the action.

1. **Setting Up the Camera for 2D**:
   - By default, Unity's camera is set up for 3D games. For a 2D game, you need to change the

camera's **Projection** from **Perspective** to **Orthographic**.

- The **Orthographic** view removes the depth effect (where objects far away appear smaller), which is important for 2D gameplay, ensuring that all objects, regardless of their position on the Z-axis, are rendered with the same scale.

To switch the camera to orthographic:

- Select the **Main Camera** in the **Hierarchy** window.
- In the **Inspector**, change the **Projection** dropdown to **Orthographic**.
- Adjust the **Size** to determine how much of the game world fits in the camera's view (larger values show more, smaller values zoom in on a smaller area).

Example:

```
csharp
CopyEdit
Camera.main.orthographic = true;  // Ensure
the camera is orthographic
Camera.main.orthographicSize = 5;     //
Adjust the orthographic size to control the
camera's zoom level
```

2. **Camera Viewport**: The **viewport** is the region of the screen in which the camera renders the game world. Unity allows you to define a specific viewport area for cameras, which can be useful for split-screen multiplayer or when you want the camera to show only a specific portion of the scene.
   - **Viewport Rect**: You can adjust the camera's viewport using the **Viewport Rect** property in the camera's **Inspector** to control how much of the screen the camera occupies. The values are between 0 and 1, where (0, 0) represents the bottom-left corner of the screen, and (1, 1) represents the top-right.

Making the Camera Follow the Player

A common feature in many 2D games is the camera that follows the player, ensuring that the character stays centered or within the view as they move. Unity allows you to achieve this by writing a simple script that continuously adjusts the camera's position based on the player's position.

1. **Basic Camera Follow**:
   - To make the camera follow the player, you'll need to update the camera's position to match the player's position, typically with some offset for

smooth movement. You can also add restrictions to the camera's movement to prevent it from going outside the boundaries of your level.

Example of a basic camera follow script:

```
csharp
CopyEdit
public Transform player;  // Reference to
the player's transform
public float smoothSpeed = 0.125f;  //
Camera movement smoothness
public Vector3 offset;  // Offset from the
player's position (e.g., to keep the player
off-center)

void LateUpdate() {
    Vector3 desiredPosition =
player.position + offset;  // Calculate the
target position
    Vector3 smoothedPosition =
Vector3.Lerp(transform.position,
desiredPosition, smoothSpeed);  // Smooth
the movement
    transform.position = smoothedPosition;
// Update the camera position
}
```

  - **offset** allows you to customize the distance between the camera and the player. For instance, if you want the camera to follow the player from behind and slightly above, you can set the offset to `(0, 5, -10)` for a 2D game.

2. **Constraining Camera Movement**:
  - In some games, it's important to prevent the camera from going outside certain boundaries (e.g., in platformers where the camera shouldn't go beyond the level's edges). To do this, you can use clamping techniques to restrict the camera's position.

Example:

```
csharp
CopyEdit
public float minX, maxX, minY, maxY;

void LateUpdate() {
    Vector3 desiredPosition =
player.position + offset;
    desiredPosition.x =
Mathf.Clamp(desiredPosition.x, minX,
maxX);  // Constrain X
    desiredPosition.y =
Mathf.Clamp(desiredPosition.y, minY,
maxY);  // Constrain Y
```

```
        transform.position = desiredPosition;
    }
```

Creating Dynamic Camera Effects (e.g., Shake, Zoom)

Dynamic camera effects can be used to enhance the player's emotional experience during critical moments in the game, such as explosions, impacts, or intense action sequences. Common effects include **camera shake** and **camera zoom**.

1. **Camera Shake**:
   - A **camera shake** effect creates a sense of impact or excitement by rapidly shifting the camera's position in random directions for a short duration.

   Example of a simple camera shake script:

```
csharp
CopyEdit
public float shakeAmount = 0.1f;  // Shake
intensity
public float shakeDuration = 0.5f;  // How
long the shake lasts

private Vector3 originalPosition;

void Start() {
```

```
    originalPosition = transform.position;
// Store the camera's original position
}

void Update() {
    if (shakeDuration > 0) {
        transform.position =
originalPosition + Random.insideUnitSphere
* shakeAmount;  // Apply shake effect
        shakeDuration -= Time.deltaTime;
// Decrease shake duration over time
    } else {
        transform.position =
originalPosition;  // Reset the camera
position
    }
}

public void TriggerShake() {
    shakeDuration = 0.5f;  // Reset shake
duration
}
```

- You can trigger the shake effect when certain events occur, like when the player gets hit or during an explosion.

2. **Camera Zoom**:
    - You can change the camera's **orthographic size** to zoom in or out, which can help emphasize

certain events or provide a different perspective during gameplay.

Example of a zoom-in and zoom-out effect:

```
csharp
CopyEdit
public float zoomInSize = 3f;  // Zoom-in
size
public float zoomOutSize = 5f;  // Default
zoom-out size
public float zoomSpeed = 2f;  // Speed at
which to zoom in/out

void Update() {
    if (Input.GetKey(KeyCode.Z)) {  // Zoom
in
        Camera.main.orthographicSize      =
Mathf.Lerp(Camera.main.orthographicSize,
zoomInSize, zoomSpeed * Time.deltaTime);
    } else {  // Zoom out
        Camera.main.orthographicSize      =
Mathf.Lerp(Camera.main.orthographicSize,
zoomOutSize, zoomSpeed * Time.deltaTime);
    }
}
```

- Zooming can be used to focus on a particular area or action, such as when a player enters a combat scenario or when exploring a detailed section of the map.

Summary

In this chapter, we've learned how to set up and manage the **camera** in a 2D game, including how to make the camera **follow the player** for smooth gameplay. We also explored how to add dynamic **camera effects** such as **shake** and **zoom**, which can be used to enhance gameplay and create memorable moments for the player.

By understanding how to control the camera, you can tailor the player's experience and provide more engaging, interactive gameplay. Whether it's keeping the player centered on the screen, adding dramatic effects during intense moments, or offering a different perspective with zooming, the camera is a crucial tool in shaping how your game is perceived.

CHAPTER 16

OPTIMIZING PERFORMANCE

As you develop your game, ensuring that it runs smoothly is critical for providing a good player experience, especially for users with varying hardware capabilities. Poor performance—such as low frame rates, long loading times, or unresponsive gameplay—can quickly drive players away. In this chapter, we'll cover **basic performance optimization techniques** in Unity, strategies for **reducing draw calls and managing resources**, and how to use **profiling tools** to check and improve your game's performance.

Basic Performance Optimization Techniques in Unity

1. **Use Efficient Assets**:
    - Ensure that the assets you're using (textures, models, sounds, etc.) are optimized for performance. For example, textures should be compressed and resized to the appropriate resolution for your game's needs. Unnecessarily large textures can drastically reduce performance, especially on lower-end devices.

   - **Texture Atlases**: Combine multiple smaller textures into one large texture (a **texture atlas**) to minimize texture switching. Unity can then use the atlas to draw multiple objects in a single batch, reducing draw calls.

2. **Optimize Game Objects**:
   - Reducing the number of **GameObjects** in your scene can improve performance. Avoid creating unnecessary objects or leaving unused ones in the scene, as each GameObject incurs overhead in terms of memory and processing.
   - If you have static objects (objects that do not move or change), mark them as **static** in Unity's inspector. Unity can optimize static objects for better performance.
3. **Efficient Use of Physics**:
   - Physics calculations can be expensive. To optimize, use Unity's **2D Physics** over 3D Physics when possible, and avoid using excessive **rigidbodies** in your scene. If an object doesn't need physics interactions, remove the rigidbody and collider components.
   - Use **Layer-based collision detection** to ensure that only relevant objects interact with each other physically.
4. **Lighting Optimization**:

- **Baked lighting**: Use baked lighting instead of dynamic lighting whenever possible, especially for static objects. This reduces the performance cost of real-time lighting calculations.
- Minimize the number of real-time lights in your scene, as they can be computationally expensive. Use **light culling** to ensure that only visible lights are active.

5. **Level of Detail (LOD)**:
   - Use **Level of Detail (LOD)** to dynamically reduce the complexity of 3D models as they get farther away from the camera. Unity supports LOD systems, which automatically swap higher-detail models for lower-detail ones at a distance.

Reducing Draw Calls and Managing Resources

Draw calls are one of the most significant factors affecting performance in Unity. Each time Unity renders something, it makes a **draw call**. Minimizing draw calls is critical for maintaining a high frame rate.

1. **Combine Meshes**:
   - **Mesh combining** allows you to combine multiple meshes into a single mesh, reducing the number of draw calls. Unity's **Static Batching** and

Dynamic Batching can automatically combine static and dynamic objects into fewer draw calls.

- However, **Static Batching** only works for static objects. To combine dynamic objects, you may need to implement custom mesh combining techniques or use the **Mesh.CombineMeshes()** function in code.

Example of combining meshes:

```
csharp
CopyEdit
MeshFilter[] meshFilters =
GetComponentsInChildren<MeshFilter>();
CombineInstance[] combine = new
CombineInstance[meshFilters.Length];

for (int i = 0; i < meshFilters.Length;
i++) {
    combine[i].mesh =
meshFilters[i].sharedMesh;
    combine[i].transform =
meshFilters[i].transform.localToWorldMatr
ix;
}

Mesh combinedMesh = new Mesh();
combinedMesh.CombineMeshes(combine);
```

```
GetComponent<MeshFilter>().mesh =
combinedMesh;
```

2. **Use Object Pooling**:
   - Rather than creating and destroying objects frequently (which is costly), use an **object pool** to reuse objects. Object pooling is a pattern that keeps objects in memory, enabling the game to quickly recycle them instead of instantiating and destroying them repeatedly.
   - Common examples of object pooling include bullets, enemies, or projectiles.

Example of a basic object pool:

```
csharp
CopyEdit
public class ObjectPool : MonoBehaviour {
    public GameObject prefab;
    public int poolSize = 10;
    private Queue<GameObject> pool = new
Queue<GameObject>();

    void Start() {
        for (int i = 0; i < poolSize; i++)
{
            GameObject obj =
Instantiate(prefab);
            obj.SetActive(false);
```

```
            pool.Enqueue(obj);
        }
    }

    public GameObject GetObject() {
        if (pool.Count > 0) {
            GameObject obj =
pool.Dequeue();
            obj.SetActive(true);
            return obj;
        } else {
            return null;
        }
    }

    public void ReturnObject(GameObject
obj) {
        obj.SetActive(false);
        pool.Enqueue(obj);
    }
}
```

3. **Texture Atlases and Sprite Sheets**:
   - Use **sprite sheets** for 2D games to combine multiple images into a single texture atlas. This reduces texture switching during rendering and improves performance.

- Unity's **Sprite Packer** can be used to automate this process, packing sprites into one texture atlas dynamically.

4. **Avoid Overuse of Transparent Objects**:
    - Transparent objects are expensive to render in Unity. Try to avoid using transparency excessively, especially in complex scenes. If possible, use **opaque objects** and adjust the alpha values only when needed.

Profiling Tools for Checking Game Performance

Unity provides a set of profiling tools that allow you to analyze and monitor the performance of your game. These tools help you identify bottlenecks and areas where optimization can make the most impact.

1. **Unity Profiler**:
    - The **Unity Profiler** is one of the most powerful tools for monitoring performance in real-time. It provides detailed information on various aspects of your game, including CPU, GPU, memory usage, rendering time, and more.
    - To open the Profiler, go to **Window > Analysis > Profiler**. The Profiler will display various

graphs and metrics that allow you to pinpoint areas where performance is lagging.

Key sections of the Profiler:

- **CPU Usage**: Shows how much processing power is used by various systems in your game (e.g., physics, AI, rendering).
- **Memory Usage**: Displays memory allocation and usage, helping you identify if there are memory leaks or inefficient memory usage.
- **Rendering**: Provides information about draw calls, the number of rendered objects, and GPU performance.

2. **Frame Debugger**:
   - The **Frame Debugger** in Unity allows you to inspect how the rendering process happens frame by frame. It shows all draw calls and helps you understand which objects and effects are taking up the most time during rendering.
   - To open the Frame Debugger, go to **Window > Analysis > Frame Debugger**. This tool is especially helpful when trying to optimize draw calls and reduce GPU workload.
3. **Memory Profiler**:
   - The **Memory Profiler** gives you detailed insights into your game's memory usage. It allows you to

    inspect the memory allocated by textures, meshes, sounds, and other assets, helping you find areas where you can reduce memory usage.
  - You can access it via **Window > Analysis > Memory**.

4. **Statistics Window**:
   - The **Statistics** window (available in the Game view) gives you a quick overview of key performance metrics, such as frame rate, draw calls, and more.
   - To open it, click the **Stats** button in the Game view. This is a great tool for quick performance checks during development.
5. **External Profiling Tools**:
   - Tools like **Xcode Instruments** (for macOS), **Android Profiler**, or **Visual Studio Profiler** can also be used to track performance on specific devices and platforms. They offer deeper insights into platform-specific issues.

Summary

Optimizing performance is essential for creating a smooth and enjoyable gaming experience. In this chapter, we've covered key techniques to improve performance, such as reducing draw calls, managing resources efficiently, and using object pooling. We also explored various **profiling tools** within Unity, like the **Profiler**, **Frame Debugger**, and **Memory Profiler**, which help you identify bottlenecks and areas for improvement. By regularly using these tools and applying the optimization techniques discussed, you can ensure that your game runs efficiently on a wide range of devices, providing a better experience for your players.

CHAPTER 17

DEBUGGING AND TROUBLESHOOTING

Debugging is a crucial skill in game development. As you work on your project, you'll inevitably encounter issues—whether it's a bug in your code, an asset not displaying correctly, or a gameplay mechanic that's not working as expected. Learning how to effectively debug and troubleshoot problems will save you time, reduce frustration, and help you deliver a polished game. In this chapter, we'll dive into the key aspects of **debugging and troubleshooting in Unity**, focusing on using **Unity's console and debugging tools**, identifying and fixing **common scripting errors**, and efficient **problem-solving strategies**.

Using Unity's Console and Debugging Tools

Unity provides a set of tools designed specifically for debugging and troubleshooting your game. Understanding how to use these tools efficiently can help you quickly identify the root cause of problems.

1. **Unity Console**:

- The **Console** in Unity is your first line of defense when it comes to identifying errors and warnings. It shows messages related to your game, including errors, warnings, and logs generated during runtime.
- You can access the Console by going to **Window > General > Console** or by pressing `Ctrl+Shift+C` (Windows) or `Cmd+Shift+C` (Mac).
- The Console shows a few key elements:
  - **Errors**: Critical issues that prevent your game from running properly.
  - **Warnings**: Potential issues that may not break your game but could lead to unexpected behavior.
  - **Logs**: Informational messages that you print to the console using `Debug.Log()`.

2. **Debugging with `Debug.Log()`, `Debug.Warning()`, and `Debug.Error()`:**
   - Unity provides three primary methods to print messages to the Console:
     - **`Debug.Log()`**: Use this for general information or to confirm that specific parts of your code are being executed.

- **`Debug.LogWarning()`**: Use this to indicate potential issues that are not errors but may require attention.
- **`Debug.LogError()`**: Use this to highlight errors that must be addressed immediately.

Example:

```
csharp
CopyEdit
Debug.Log("Player health: " + playerHealth);
Debug.LogWarning("Enemy AI is not reacting correctly.");
Debug.LogError("Player object not found!");
```

3. **Breakpoints and the Unity Debugger**:
   - **Breakpoints** allow you to pause your game at a specific line of code and step through it to examine its behavior. This is useful for pinpointing exactly where things go wrong in your game's logic.
   - You can set breakpoints directly in **Visual Studio** or any other IDE you are using, provided you have the Unity integration installed. When you hit the breakpoint, the game pauses, and you can

inspect variables, check the call stack, and evaluate expressions.

- To set a breakpoint, simply click next to the line number in your IDE. When you run the game, the debugger will pause at that point, allowing you to step through the code line by line.

4. **Inspecting Variables at Runtime**:
   - Unity's **Inspector** window allows you to see the values of variables in real-time as the game runs. This is helpful when you want to check if a variable's value is behaving as expected.
   - You can add **[SerializeField]** before private variables to make them visible in the Inspector during runtime. If you need to watch variables more closely, you can also use **Debug.Log()** to print variable values directly to the Console.

Identifying and Fixing Common Scripting Errors

During development, you'll encounter a variety of errors. These can range from syntax mistakes to logical errors that are harder to spot. Below are some common types of errors you may encounter and strategies to fix them.

1. **Syntax Errors**:

- **Description**: These errors occur when you've written code that doesn't follow the correct syntax of the C# language. For example, missing semicolons, unmatched parentheses, or improper use of keywords.
- **How to Fix**: The Unity Console will usually highlight these errors with a red message indicating the line number where the error occurred. Carefully check the line for missing punctuation or incorrect syntax.

2. **Null Reference Exceptions**:
   - **Description**: This is one of the most common errors in Unity. It occurs when you try to access a method or property on an object that has not been initialized (i.e., it's **null**).
   - **How to Fix**: Always ensure that an object is properly initialized before accessing it. Check if an object is null using conditional statements, like so:

```
csharp
CopyEdit
if (myObject != null) {
    myObject.DoSomething();
}
```

3. **Index Out of Range Errors**:

- Description: This occurs when you try to access an element in an array or list that doesn't exist (for example, accessing index `5` in a list that only has `3` items).
- **How to Fix**: Always make sure you're accessing valid indices in arrays or lists by checking the length beforehand:

```
csharp
CopyEdit
if (index < myList.Count) {
    var item = myList[index];
}
```

4. **Infinite Loops and Performance Issues**:
   - **Description**: Infinite loops (e.g., `while(true)`) can freeze your game, and excessive loops can slow down performance.
   - **How to Fix**: Be mindful of loop conditions and consider breaking out of loops after a certain number of iterations to avoid performance degradation. You can also use **Debug.Log()** to ensure your loops are executing as expected.
5. **Incorrect Component References**:
   - **Description**: Frequently, you'll see errors related to missing or incorrectly assigned components.

For instance, trying to access a `Rigidbody2D` on an object that doesn't have it attached.

- **How to Fix**: Double-check the component references in the Unity Inspector. If a component is missing, add it, or add code that checks whether the component exists before using it:

```
csharp
CopyEdit
Rigidbody2D rb =
GetComponent<Rigidbody2D>();
if (rb != null) {
    rb.AddForce(Vector2.up);
} else {
    Debug.LogError("Rigidbody2D
component not found!");
}
```

Efficient Problem-Solving Strategies for Game Development

1. **Divide and Conquer**:
   - When encountering an issue, try to isolate the problem. Start by determining whether the issue is with your **code**, **assets**, or **Unity settings**. This helps you narrow down your search.

- o If the issue involves complex systems (like physics, AI, etc.), break them down into smaller sections and test each part separately.

2. **Reproduce the Issue Consistently**:
   - o To effectively debug, you need to reproduce the problem consistently. If the error happens randomly, try to identify specific conditions or actions that trigger the bug.
   - o Once you've reproduced the error, use breakpoints, logs, and the Inspector to track down the source.
3. **Ask for Help**:
   - o Sometimes, a fresh set of eyes can catch things you may have missed. Don't hesitate to ask for help from colleagues or the online developer community.
   - o Unity's **forums** and **Stack Overflow** are great places to ask for advice and share your code snippets. Make sure to describe the problem clearly and provide relevant details.
4. **Use Version Control**:
   - o To avoid losing progress when debugging, always use a version control system like **Git**. This allows you to easily revert to previous versions of your game if something goes wrong while debugging.

    - Version control also allows you to experiment with fixes in isolated branches and merge changes once you're confident in your solution.

5. **Test on Multiple Devices**:
    - Sometimes, bugs only appear on specific devices or platforms. Always test your game on multiple platforms (PC, mobile, etc.) to ensure that your code works across different configurations.
    - Use Unity's **Build Settings** and **Player Settings** to build and test your game on different platforms.

Summary

Debugging and troubleshooting are essential parts of game development, and knowing how to effectively use Unity's debugging tools will save you a lot of time. By utilizing the **Console**, **breakpoints**, **Inspector**, and **logging methods**, you can identify and fix issues in your game. Understanding common scripting errors and adopting efficient problem-solving strategies will make debugging more manageable. With these skills, you'll be able to overcome obstacles and deliver a polished and bug-free game.

CHAPTER 18

BUILDING FOR MULTIPLE PLATFORMS

Once you've developed your game in Unity, the next crucial step is **building** it for different platforms. Unity supports exporting to a wide range of platforms, including **PC**, **macOS**, **Linux**, **iOS**, **Android**, and even consoles like the **Nintendo Switch** and **PlayStation**. The key to successfully exporting your game is making sure that it works seamlessly across all these platforms, each with its own requirements and unique user experiences. In this chapter, we'll explore how to export your Unity game for different platforms, handle **screen resolutions and aspect ratios**, and adjust **input methods** for various devices.

Exporting a Unity Game to Different Platforms (PC, Mobile, etc.)

Unity's built-in tools make it relatively straightforward to export your game to multiple platforms. The process involves selecting the target platform and adjusting settings to optimize the game for that environment.

1. **Unity Build Settings**:

   - To begin the process, open the **Build Settings** window in Unity by going to **File > Build Settings**. Here, you'll see a list of platforms you can export to, including **PC, Mac, Linux Standalone**, **iOS**, **Android**, **WebGL**, and more.
   - Select the platform you want to build for, and click on **Switch Platform**. Unity will configure the project for that specific platform. Some platforms may require additional software or SDKs installed (e.g., Xcode for iOS, Android Studio for Android).
2. **PC / Mac / Linux Standalone**:
   - For desktop platforms like **Windows** or **macOS**, you can export your game as a standalone executable.
   - In the **Build Settings** window, select **PC, Mac & Linux Standalone** and choose the target operating system (e.g., Windows or macOS).
   - Once you hit **Build**, Unity compiles your game and creates an executable file that you can share or distribute.
   - **Optimization Tip**: For desktop games, make sure to enable or disable features such as **full-screen mode** and **resolution scaling** based on the player's device specifications.
3. **Mobile Platforms (iOS and Android)**:

- Exporting for **iOS** or **Android** requires additional setup. You need the respective SDKs (iOS requires **Xcode**, Android requires **Android SDK/NDK**).
- **iOS Export**: For **iOS**, you will need to ensure that your game is configured to work with **iOS-specific settings** in Unity, including adjusting the **App icons**, **Splash Screens**, and **Xcode configurations**.
- **Android Export**: For **Android**, you'll need to configure settings like the **minimum API level**, **keystore for signing**, and **resolution scaling**.
- Once the build settings are configured, Unity can generate the necessary files to be uploaded to the **App Store** or **Google Play Store**.

4. **Console Platforms**:
    - Unity also supports consoles like **PlayStation**, **Xbox**, and **Nintendo Switch**, but building for these platforms often requires developer access to their respective SDKs and specific hardware.
    - You will need to ensure compliance with the platform's requirements, such as control schemes, achievements, and network integration.
    - Some consoles, like **PlayStation**, also require special licensing and certification before you can distribute your game.

5. **WebGL**:
   - **WebGL** allows you to run your Unity game directly in a web browser. When building for **WebGL,** Unity compiles your game into JavaScript and HTML5.
   - This is ideal for games that you want to play on a website without needing to download an executable.
   - However, WebGL has limitations, such as reduced graphics performance and limited access to system resources, so be sure to test your game thoroughly in this format.

Handling Screen Resolutions and Aspect Ratios

Games are played on a variety of devices, each with different screen resolutions and aspect ratios. Properly managing how your game scales to these different screens ensures that it looks good and is playable on all devices.

1. **Resolution and Aspect Ratio Considerations**:
   - Different devices have different screen resolutions (e.g., a **phone** may have a **1080x1920** resolution, while a **PC monitor** may have **1920x1080**). Some devices, like **iPads** or

  - **Android tablets**, may also have unique aspect ratios.
  - Unity provides tools to handle screen resolutions and aspect ratios. You can configure your game to automatically scale or crop to fit different devices.
2. **Canvas Scaler for UI**:
   - The **Canvas Scaler** component in Unity allows you to control how the UI elements scale across different screen sizes. You can set it to **Constant Pixel Size**, **Scale With Screen Size**, or **Constant Physical Size**.
   - For most cases, **Scale With Screen Size** is recommended, especially for mobile devices. This ensures that UI elements scale according to the screen resolution, maintaining consistency across devices.
3. **Aspect Ratio Fitting**:
   - Unity includes tools to manage different aspect ratios. You can specify which aspect ratios your game supports (e.g., 16:9, 4:3, 21:9) and then decide how to handle aspect ratio mismatches.
   - You can use the **Camera's Viewport Rect** to adjust how your camera's view is cropped or letterboxed on different screen ratios. This is

particularly useful when you want to ensure that critical elements in the game are always visible.

4. **Letterboxing and Pillarboxing**:
   - To handle screen ratios that don't match the intended aspect ratio (e.g., 4:3 on a 16:9 screen), you can use letterboxing (black bars on top and bottom) or pillarboxing (black bars on the sides) to preserve the game's layout and prevent it from becoming stretched or squished.
   - You can also choose to **zoom** the camera to fit the screen without introducing black bars, but this might cause parts of the game to be cut off if the aspect ratio mismatch is too large.

Adjusting Input Methods for Different Devices (Keyboard, Touch)

Input handling varies greatly between devices. A game designed for a **PC** will likely rely on **keyboard and mouse input**, while a game for a **mobile device** will use **touch input**. Unity makes it easy to manage different input types, but you need to ensure your game responds appropriately across platforms.

1. **Input for PC**:
   - For **PC** games, you'll be handling input primarily through the **keyboard** and **mouse**. Unity

provides the `Input` class, which lets you capture inputs from these devices.

- For example:

```
csharp
CopyEdit
float horizontal =
Input.GetAxis("Horizontal"); //
Arrow keys or WASD
if (Input.GetKeyDown(KeyCode.Space))
{
    Jump();
}
```

- You can also detect **mouse clicks** and mouse position using `Input.GetMouseButtonDown()` and `Input.mousePosition`.

2. **Input for Mobile (Touch)**:
   - For **mobile games**, Unity's **Touch API** lets you detect touch input. The basic structure of touch input involves capturing the number of touches and their positions:

```
csharp
CopyEdit
if (Input.touchCount > 0) {
    Touch touch = Input.GetTouch(0);
```

```
    Vector2     touchPosition     =
touch.position;
    // Handle touch input here
}
```

- Mobile devices don't have a **mouse cursor**, so you'll rely on touches or gestures to interact with the game. Be sure to adjust your UI and controls to accommodate touch-based input.

3. **Handling Multiple Input Methods**:
   - Many games need to work with both **keyboard/mouse** and **touch** input, depending on the platform. Unity allows you to create flexible controls that can adapt to either input method. You can check for the platform and adjust input handling accordingly:

```
csharp
CopyEdit
if (Application.isMobilePlatform) {
    // Handle mobile-specific input
(touch, accelerometer, etc.)
} else {
    // Handle keyboard/mouse input
}
```

4. **Joystick/Gamepad Support**:

  - If you're building a game that will support **gamepads** or **joysticks** (common for console games), Unity automatically detects input from most controllers. You can use the `Input.GetAxis()` or `Input.GetButtonDown()` methods to handle gamepad input, and Unity will map it to the controller's buttons or axes.

Summary

Building a Unity game for multiple platforms can seem like a daunting task, but with Unity's built-in tools, it's easier than ever to export your game to different devices. By carefully handling **screen resolutions**, **aspect ratios**, and **input methods**, you can ensure your game looks great and plays well on a variety of platforms. Whether you're targeting **PC**, **mobile devices**, or **consoles**, Unity provides the flexibility you need to bring your game to life across all platforms. Keep testing your game on different devices and be prepared to tweak your settings to provide the best possible experience for every player.

CHAPTER 19

GAME MONETIZATION AND IN-APP PURCHASES

You've got a playable game. Now comes the part many developers overlook until the end—**monetization**. It's not just about slapping ads or price tags on things. You need a plan that respects players, sustains the game, and doesn't ruin the experience. In this chapter, we'll break down monetization strategies, show how to implement **in-app purchases (IAPs)** and **ads** in Unity, and explain how to use **analytics** to understand your players and fine-tune your monetization tactics.

Introduction to Game Monetization Strategies

There are three broad approaches to monetizing games, especially on mobile and web platforms:

1. **Free-to-Play (F2P) with In-App Purchases (IAPs)**
    - The game is free to download and play, but players can pay for extra content like new levels, cosmetic items, or currency.
    - Works well for mobile games or any casual audience.

  - Key challenge: striking the balance between generosity and making players want to spend without feeling forced.

2. **Ad-Supported Games**
   - You integrate ads (banners, interstitials, rewarded videos) and earn based on impressions or clicks.
   - Best for games with high retention and frequent sessions.
   - Make sure you don't overload the player with ads; reward them instead (e.g., "Watch an ad to earn double coins").
3. **Premium Model**
   - The game has a one-time purchase price.
   - More common on PC or console. Less common on mobile unless you've got a strong hook or fanbase.
   - Cleaner experience for players, but you'll need solid marketing to convince people upfront.

You can also mix these models (e.g., a free game with optional ads and purchasable cosmetic content). The key is to **not annoy players** into quitting.

Adding In-App Purchases or Ads in Unity

Unity provides services and integrations to easily add monetization to your project. The most popular tools are **Unity IAP** and **Unity Ads**, both of which are available through the Unity Services system.

Setting Up Unity IAP (In-App Purchasing)

Unity's IAP package helps you handle purchases across multiple platforms without writing separate code for each one.

1. **Install Unity IAP**:
    - Go to **Window > Package Manager**, search for **In-App Purchasing**, and install it.
    - Then, go to **Services > In-App Purchasing** and turn it on.
2. **Set Up Your Products**:
    - Define your products in the Unity Dashboard (e.g., coin packs, skins, level unlocks).
    - Give each item a unique **product ID** that matches what's in the App Store / Google Play.
3. **Sample IAP Code**:

```
csharp
CopyEdit
using UnityEngine.Purchasing;
```

```
public class IAPManager : MonoBehaviour,
IStoreListener {
    public void
OnInitialized(IStoreController controller,
IExtensionProvider extensions) {
        Debug.Log("IAP initialized");
    }

    public void OnPurchaseComplete(Product
product) {
        if (product.definition.id ==
"coin_pack_100") {
            // Grant coins to player
        }
    }

    public void OnPurchaseFailed(Product
product, PurchaseFailureReason reason) {
        Debug.Log($"Purchase failed:
{reason}");
    }
}
```

- You'll need to handle edge cases like failed transactions, duplicate purchases, or restoring purchases on iOS.

Adding Ads Using Unity Ads

Unity Ads is the quickest way to monetize players without making them pay upfront. It's ideal for mobile games.

1. **Enable Unity Ads**:
   - In the Unity Dashboard, go to **Monetization** and enable Unity Ads for your project.
   - Install the **Advertisement** package from Package Manager.
2. **Types of Ads**:
   - **Interstitial** (appears at transitions like level end).
   - **Banner** (discreet ads that stay on screen).
   - **Rewarded Video** (players watch an ad in exchange for a reward).
3. **Sample Ad Code**:

```
csharp
CopyEdit
using UnityEngine.Advertisements;

public class AdManager : MonoBehaviour {
    public void ShowRewardedAd() {
        if
(Advertisement.IsReady("rewardedVideo")) {

Advertisement.Show("rewardedVideo",    new
ShowOptions {
```

```
                    resultCallback = result =>
{
                        if      (result      ==
ShowResult.Finished) {
                            // Give reward to
player
                        }
                    }
                });
            }
        }
}
```

4. **Best Practices**:
    - Always give players the option to skip or refuse.
    - Rewarded ads should feel optional, not required to progress.
    - Track player engagement. If ad frequency is high and playtime is dropping, scale back.

Analytics and Tracking Player Behavior

You can't improve what you don't measure. **Game analytics** help you understand how people play your game, what they like, where they quit, and what makes them spend money.

Unity Analytics

Unity's built-in analytics give you quick insights into player behavior.

1. **Enable Analytics**:
   - Go to **Services > Analytics** and toggle it on.
2. **Track Custom Events**:

```
csharp
CopyEdit
using UnityEngine.Analytics;
using System.Collections.Generic;

Analytics.CustomEvent("level_complete",
new Dictionary<string, object> {
    { "level", 5 },
    { "time_taken", 120 }
});
```

3. **What You Should Track**:
   - Session length
   - Levels completed
   - Items purchased
   - Ads watched
   - Drop-off points (where players quit)
4. **Third-Party Tools**:

  - Consider using tools like **Firebase**, **GameAnalytics**, or **Amplitude** if you want deeper analytics, heatmaps, or A/B testing.
5. **Using Data Wisely**:
  - Don't track everything—track what helps you answer questions.
  - Use data to balance difficulty, improve tutorials, or tweak monetization points.
  - If players leave after a certain level, maybe the difficulty spikes or rewards drop off too quickly.

Summary

If you want to make money from your game, it needs more than flashy graphics or great mechanics. It needs thoughtful monetization baked in from the start—*without frustrating players*. Unity makes it easy to implement **IAPs**, show **ads**, and gather **analytics** to improve your strategy. Just don't let monetization get in the way of a good game. The goal is to build something people *want* to pay for—or watch an ad for—not something that feels like a cash grab. Be smart. Be fair. Let the data guide you.

CHAPTER 20

MULTIPLAYER CONCEPTS IN UNITY

Multiplayer can make a simple game way more engaging—or turn it into a buggy mess if you don't plan it right. This chapter gives you a no-nonsense rundown of what it actually takes to add multiplayer features to a Unity game. Whether it's just two players competing locally or a full online battle system, you'll need to understand how data flows between players, what libraries are available, and how to keep everything in sync without lagging into oblivion.

Basics of Networking and Multiplayer in Unity

At its core, multiplayer means synchronizing the game state between two or more players. When one player does something—like moving, jumping, or shooting—that action needs to be seen by everyone else, as close to real-time as possible.

Key multiplayer concepts:

- **Client**: A player's game instance.

- **Server**: The central authority that controls the game state and validates actions.
- **Host**: A hybrid that acts as both server and client.
- **RPC (Remote Procedure Call)**: Code triggered on one client or the server that gets executed somewhere else.

You'll also need to handle:

- **Lag compensation** (because the internet isn't instant),
- **Cheat prevention** (don't trust clients too much),
- **Matchmaking**, and
- **Session management** (players joining/leaving).

Introduction to Unity's Networking Libraries

Unity used to have a built-in solution called **UNet**, but that's been deprecated. Now, there are a few modern choices:

1. **Unity Netcode for GameObjects (NGO)** – Unity's official networking framework. Good for small-scale real-time games.
    - Built-in support for host-client architecture.
    - Works with Unity Transport (for data transmission).
    - Great if you're already using Unity's GameObject system.
2. **Photon (PUN 2 / Fusion)** – Third-party, very popular.

    - Quick to get up and running.
    - Handles matchmaking, room management, and more.
    - Free for small-scale use; charges based on concurrent users.
3. **Mirror** – Community-maintained fork of UNet.
    - Easy to learn if you're familiar with UNet.
    - Very flexible but requires more manual work.
    - Suitable for indie games with custom networking needs.
4. **Fish-Networking** – More advanced, designed for high-performance multiplayer (think large-scale games).

For this chapter, we'll keep it practical and use **Unity Netcode for GameObjects (NGO)**, since it's directly supported and beginner-friendly.

Setting Up a Simple Multiplayer Scene (Using Unity Netcode)

Let's say you want two players to connect and see each other move in a basic 2D arena.

Step 1: Install NGO

- Open the Package Manager.

- Add `com.unity.netcode.gameobjects` and `com.unity.transport`.

Step 2: Set Up the Network Manager

- Create an empty GameObject, name it `NetworkManager`.
- Add a `NetworkManager` component.
- Assign the transport (usually `Unity Transport`).

Step 3: Create a Player Prefab

- Make a simple 2D sprite (like a box).
- Add a `NetworkObject` component.
- Add a `NetworkTransform` to sync movement.
- Create a script that lets only the owner control it:

```
csharp
CopyEdit
using Unity.Netcode;
using UnityEngine;

public class PlayerController :
NetworkBehaviour {
    public float moveSpeed = 5f;

    void Update() {
        if (!IsOwner) return;
```

```
        float moveX = Input.GetAxis("Horizontal");
        float moveY = Input.GetAxis("Vertical");
        transform.Translate(new Vector2(moveX, moveY) * moveSpeed * Time.deltaTime);
    }
}
```

Step 4: Configure the Network Manager

- Drag your player prefab into the `NetworkManager`'s Player Prefab slot.
- Add buttons in your UI to call:
    - `StartHost()`
    - `StartClient()`
    - `StartServer()` (if needed)

Now two players can join the same scene and see each other move around. Congrats, that's multiplayer—barebones but functional.

Simple Player vs Player Mechanics

Once players can see each other, the next step is interaction—like attacking.

Add a shooting mechanic (with RPC):

```
csharp
CopyEdit
public class PlayerCombat : NetworkBehaviour {
    public GameObject bulletPrefab;
    public Transform firePoint;

    void Update() {
        if (!IsOwner) return;

        if (Input.GetKeyDown(KeyCode.Space)) {
            ShootServerRpc();
        }
    }

    [ServerRpc]
    void ShootServerRpc() {
        GameObject                bullet               =
Instantiate(bulletPrefab,    firePoint.position,
Quaternion.identity);

bullet.GetComponent<NetworkObject>().Spawn();

bullet.GetComponent<Rigidbody2D>().velocity     =
Vector2.right * 10f;
    }
}
```

Add collision detection to bullets. When a bullet hits another player, you can use ServerRpc to reduce health or trigger respawn.

Note: Never trust clients to report kills. Always validate attacks on the server side.

Things to Watch Out For

- **Latency**: Always assume a delay between action and response.
- **Synchronization**: Use NetworkVariables for things like health, position, score.
- **Cheating**: Don't let clients control important logic like scoring or win conditions.
- **Session drops**: Handle what happens if a player disconnects mid-game.

Summary

Multiplayer sounds daunting but can be broken down into manageable pieces—especially with Unity's Netcode tools. You start with a simple shared scene, sync player movement, and build from there. The core is all about **communication**: what gets sent, when, and who's allowed to say what. Whether you go peer-to-peer or client-server, always plan for bad connections, slow devices, and the inevitable edge cases. Start small, test everything, and only scale up when the basics feel rock solid.

CHAPTER 21

POLISHING YOUR GAME

Once your game is playable and technically sound, the last 10% of the work—the polish—will make or break how people respond to it. This is the point where a functional game becomes a game people enjoy. Polishing isn't just about making things look pretty. It's about tightening the screws, eliminating friction, and making the experience feel intentional.

Adding Finishing Touches: Animations, Sound, Transitions

This is where subtle enhancements matter. Every detail communicates quality, so pay attention to the small stuff.

1. Animations

- Go back through your game and find any abrupt or janky transitions (like a character snapping from idle to walk).
- Use **Animator State Machines** to blend animations smoothly.
- Add in-between frames where necessary—players notice when a punch feels off or a jump lacks anticipation.
- Consider using **animation events** to trigger sounds or effects at specific keyframes.

2. Sound Polish

- Sync sound effects to player actions—footsteps, jumping, UI clicks.
- Adjust volume levels so that nothing overpowers.
- Add ambient layers (wind, city noise, forest sounds) to breathe life into static backgrounds.
- Use an **audio mixer** to group sounds and apply effects like low-pass filters or reverb during pause menus or slow-motion events.

3. Scene Transitions

- Abrupt scene loads feel amateurish. Add fade-ins/outs, loading screens, or transition animations.
- Consider using a **transition manager script** that handles scene switching and optional loading indicators.

Balancing Gameplay and Adjusting Difficulty

Your mechanics might be in place, but if the challenge isn't right, your game will either frustrate or bore players.

1. Difficulty Curve

- Start easy, then gradually increase challenge. Introduce one new mechanic at a time.

- Use early levels as tutorials without being heavy-handed.
- Observe players: If they fail the same section repeatedly, it's probably not fun.

2. Enemy and Power Balancing

- Is your enemy AI too dumb or too perfect? Adjust detection ranges, reaction times, or behavior scripts.
- Are power-ups making players invincible too early? Reconsider placement or effects.

3. Use Variables for Tweaks

- Use serialized fields for things like health, damage, spawn rates.
- Tune these values through actual play sessions—not just guesses.

4. Playtesting

- Run your game by fresh players and *watch them play*. Don't explain.
- Take notes on where they struggle, what they enjoy, and when they get bored.
- Iterate, adjust, repeat.

Final Tweaks Before Release

This is your last checkpoint before putting your work out there. Don't rush it.

1. Clean the Project

- Delete unused assets, scripts, and scenes.
- Reorganize folders—future you will thank you.

2. Check for Bugs

- Use Unity's **Profiler** and **Debug Console**.
- Look for null references, unassigned variables, UI overlaps, etc.
- Use try-catch blocks sparingly to catch runtime issues without crashing.

3. Build Settings

- Double-check resolution, aspect ratio, and quality settings.
- Test your game on all platforms you plan to release on (desktop, mobile, WebGL, etc.).
- Configure your player settings (icon, company name, splash screen, etc.).

4. Localization and Accessibility (Optional, but worth it)

- Even if you're launching in one language, design UI to allow for expansion.
- Consider players with disabilities—can it be played without sound? Is the text readable?

5. Final Packaging

- Export your builds.
- Test the final installer or file on multiple devices.
- Don't rely on the Unity editor for your final opinion—always test actual builds.

Wrap-Up

Polishing is the point where you slow down, zoom in, and obsess over the details. This chapter isn't about reinventing anything—it's about cleaning, refining, and tightening what's already there. If development is about making something work, polishing is about making it feel right. That's the difference between "it runs" and "this is fun." So go back through every menu, every jump, every animation. Assume nothing is fine until you've personally made sure it's excellent.

CHAPTER 22

PUBLISHING YOUR GAME

After all the hard work of creating, testing, and polishing your game, the next step is releasing it to the world. This chapter covers everything you need to know about preparing your game for launch, submitting it to digital stores, and managing feedback and updates after your game goes live. A smooth release doesn't just happen; it requires careful planning and organization to ensure your game gets the attention it deserves and can be enjoyed by players around the world.

Preparing Your Game for Release

1. Game Icon and Splash Screen

- **Game Icon**: Your game icon is the first thing players will see, so it needs to be eye-catching and represent the spirit of your game. It should be clear, simple, and work well at small sizes. Most platforms will require specific resolutions for icons (e.g., 512x512 pixels for Google Play and 1024x1024 for the App Store).
- **Splash Screen**: The splash screen is the first image players see when launching your game. It's often used to

show off your logo or give the player a moment to recognize the game. Keep it brief and ensure it's not too long to avoid frustrating players. Ensure it looks great across different screen sizes, as mobile devices have varying resolutions.

2. Final Touches

- **App Description**: Write a clear and engaging description of your game for the store listing. This is often the deciding factor in whether someone downloads your game. Highlight unique features, gameplay, and why it's worth the player's time.
- **Screenshots & Videos**: Include screenshots or short videos that demonstrate your game's mechanics and visuals. These are essential for attracting potential players. Make sure to showcase exciting moments that represent the core gameplay experience.
- **App Store Optimization (ASO)**: Just like SEO for websites, ASO helps your game appear higher in search results on digital stores. Use relevant keywords in your description, title, and tags.

Packaging and Submitting to Stores

1. Exporting and Packaging Your Game Before submitting your game, you need to package it for each platform.

- **Google Play (Android)**:
  - Export your game as an APK file (Android Package).
  - In Unity, go to `File > Build Settings`, select Android, and click `Build`.
  - Make sure your game is optimized for mobile devices (check performance, controls, and UI).
  - Sign your APK with a keystore file for security.
- **App Store (iOS)**:
  - Export your game as an Xcode project from Unity.
  - Open it in Xcode, configure settings (like icons, splash screens), and ensure everything is ready.
  - Test your game thoroughly in Xcode's simulator and on real devices.
  - Submit the build to App Store Connect for review.
- **Steam (PC)**:
  - Export your game as a standalone executable (e.g., .exe for Windows).

  - Set up Steamworks, which allows you to integrate features like Steam achievements, cloud saving, and leaderboards.
  - Prepare your Steam store page with assets (icon, screenshots, trailers).
  - Submit the build through Steam's publishing tools.

2. Platform-Specific Guidelines Each platform has its own set of submission guidelines:

- **Google Play**: Follow Google's requirements for app content, privacy policies, and age ratings.
- **App Store**: Ensure your game complies with Apple's strict guidelines, particularly for UI design, content, and monetization.
- **Steam**: Steam's submission process involves Steam Direct, a platform for self-publishing, but you need to submit tax and identity verification information.

3. Build and Versioning Make sure to follow versioning conventions and ensure you don't submit incomplete builds. Always test the final version thoroughly before submitting. Use clear version numbers so players and reviewers know what to expect.

Handling Feedback and Updates After Launch

1. Managing Player Feedback Once your game is out in the wild, you'll start receiving feedback. Here's how to handle it effectively:

- **Monitor Reviews**: Keep an eye on player reviews in the app stores or platforms. Respond to negative feedback calmly and professionally, and thank players for positive reviews.
- **Use Analytics**: Platforms like Unity Analytics or third-party tools (like GameAnalytics) can help you track how players are interacting with your game. Look for areas where players are dropping off, struggling, or completing specific challenges.
- **Social Media and Forums**: Create social media channels (Twitter, Facebook, Reddit, etc.) to interact with players. Communities often have valuable insights and can help spread the word about your game.

2. Hotfixes and Patches

- After launch, it's almost inevitable that some bugs will slip through the cracks. Prioritize critical fixes (game-breaking bugs, crashes) and release hotfixes as soon as possible.

- Keep a changelog of updates and be transparent with your community. Let players know when a bug has been fixed or when new features are coming.

3. Post-Launch Updates and Content

- **Free Updates**: Add new levels, characters, or features to keep players coming back. This can also help your game stay relevant.
- **Monetized Updates**: If your game has in-app purchases or ads, consider adding new content that enhances the player's experience (e.g., skins, power-ups, new game modes). However, be careful not to disrupt the balance of the game.
- **Community Involvement**: Involve your community in post-launch development. Consider community challenges, polls, or suggestions for future updates.

4. Version Control and Backups

- Keep backups of all game builds and assets, and ensure that your development tools are updated. This helps if something goes wrong with an update or you need to roll back to a previous version.

Summary

Publishing your game is the exciting culmination of months—or even years—of work, but it's only the beginning. After release, your game needs nurturing through feedback, updates, and ongoing player engagement. This chapter covered all the crucial steps to get your game out there, from finalizing your assets to navigating the submission process across multiple platforms. By the end, you'll be well-prepared to bring your game to players, handle feedback, and keep improving it long after it's launched. Happy publishing!

CHAPTER 23

POST-LAUNCH SUPPORT AND COMMUNITY BUILDING

Releasing a game isn't the end of the journey—it's just the beginning of an ongoing process. After the launch, the real work begins in maintaining player engagement, addressing issues, and building a loyal community. This chapter will guide you through managing post-launch support, handling updates and bug fixes, and creating a thriving community that will keep your game alive long after it's been launched.

Managing Community Feedback and Support Channels

1. Importance of Listening to Your Community Your players are your best source of information after your game has been released. They'll encounter issues, have suggestions, and share their experiences, which can help you improve the game. By actively listening to your community, you show that you care about their experience, which fosters loyalty.

2. Setting Up Support Channels To manage feedback and provide effective support, you need to set up dedicated channels where players can easily reach you. These could include:

- **Official Website or Forum**: A dedicated space for FAQs, troubleshooting guides, and a community space for players to share ideas or problems.
- **Social Media**: Create accounts on Twitter, Facebook, Reddit, or Discord to directly interact with your community. Social media is a quick way to share updates and engage with players.
- **Email Support**: Set up an official email for bug reports and technical support. This helps centralize feedback and keeps communication formal and organized.
- **In-Game Support Options**: Integrating a feedback or help button within the game itself allows players to report bugs or ask for support without leaving the game.

3. Organizing and Responding to Feedback

- **Centralized Tracking Tools**: Use tools like Trello, Jira, or GitHub Issues to organize feedback, bug reports, and feature requests. This way, you can prioritize what needs fixing and keep track of ongoing issues.
- **Timely Responses**: While you may not be able to address every concern immediately, make sure to acknowledge player feedback. Even a simple response like, "We're aware of the issue and working on it," helps build trust with your community.
- **Transparency**: Be honest about what is possible and what might take longer. Let players know your roadmap

and set expectations for when they can expect updates or fixes.

Handling Updates and Bug Fixes After Launch

1. Prioritizing Critical Bug Fixes Post-launch, your game is likely to encounter new bugs and issues that weren't caught during development or testing. Some bugs may be game-breaking, while others might be minor annoyances. The key is to prioritize fixes based on severity:

- **Critical Bugs**: These are issues that stop the game from functioning properly, such as crashes, broken controls, or in-game progression problems. These should be addressed immediately in a patch.
- **Minor Bugs**: These could be visual glitches, slight UI misalignments, or rare, non-disruptive bugs. While still important to fix, these can be tackled in smaller updates or future patches.
- **Feature Enhancements**: After addressing bugs, consider adding new features or improving existing ones based on player feedback. This keeps your game fresh and exciting.

2. Rolling Out Updates Once the fixes and new features are ready, it's time to release an update. Depending on the platform, updates can be submitted in various ways:

- **Mobile (Google Play/App Store)**: For mobile games, you'll need to submit updates through the respective store portals. Each update will undergo a review process, so keep track of submission times and be prepared for potential delays.
- **PC (Steam)**: Steam makes updating your game relatively simple through the Steamworks platform. You can push updates easily to players, but remember to provide patch notes so players know what has changed.
- **Web (WebGL/Browser Games)**: For web games, updates can often be deployed instantly by uploading a new version of the game to the hosting server. Ensure you notify players of any new changes.

3. Communicating with Your Players Every update should be accompanied by clear and detailed patch notes. This transparency informs your players about what has been fixed, what new features have been added, and what to expect in the future. A well-written patch note can also re-engage players who may have stopped playing due to earlier issues. Keep your community in the loop with:

- **Patch Notes**: Include both technical changes (bug fixes) and user-facing changes (new content, features, etc.).
- **Announcements**: Use social media or in-game pop-ups to notify players about the update and encourage them to try out new content.

Building a Community Around Your Game

1. Why Community Matters A strong, engaged community can help your game thrive long after its initial release. They provide free marketing through word-of-mouth, give valuable feedback on game features, and can even contribute to the game's longevity through mods or fan content. A passionate community also adds to the fun of game development, as you get to interact with your most dedicated players.

2. Engaging Your Community Building and maintaining a community requires constant attention, but it's well worth the effort. Here are some ways to keep your players engaged:

- **Discord Server**: This is one of the best tools for fostering a community. Create a server where players can chat, report issues, and interact with one another. You can create different channels for discussions, game strategies, fan art, bug reports, etc. It also allows you to hold events or giveaways.
- **Regular Communication**: Stay in touch with your community by posting regularly on social media and your forum. Share development progress, upcoming features, or interesting behind-the-scenes content to keep them invested in your game.

- **User-Generated Content**: Encourage players to create and share their own content—be it mods, fan art, or strategies. You can even hold contests to promote user-generated content. Highlighting fan-made content on your social media or in-game is a great way to reward and inspire your community.

3. Hosting Events and Competitions

- **In-Game Events**: These can range from limited-time challenges to special holiday-themed events. These keep players coming back to the game and create a sense of excitement.
- **Competitions and Tournaments**: If your game involves competitive gameplay, hosting tournaments or competitions can engage your community and create a deeper connection with the game. Offering rewards for winners (such as in-game items or recognition) can also increase participation.
- **Live Streams and Q&A**: Hosting regular live streams or Q&A sessions with the development team can give players a chance to interact with you directly. This transparency builds trust and shows that you value their input.

4. Growing Your Community

- **Influencers and Streamers**: Reach out to influencers and streamers who might be interested in playing your game. Their audiences can significantly boost visibility. However, don't just send a generic message—personalize your outreach and explain why your game would be a good fit for their content.
- **Referral Programs**: Consider implementing referral programs or rewards for players who invite their friends. This helps spread your game naturally through word-of-mouth.
- **Reddit and Forums**: Platforms like Reddit or specialized forums are great places to connect with potential players. Participate in game development or gaming-related subreddits to share progress, announce updates, or answer questions.

Summary

Post-launch support is an essential part of game development. Managing community feedback, handling updates, and maintaining an engaged player base are just as important as the development process itself. By setting up proper support channels, listening to your community, and regularly updating the game with bug fixes and new content, you can ensure your game's long-term success. Building a community around your game requires time, patience, and genuine interaction, but with the right approach, it can become one of your game's most valuable assets.

CHAPTER 24

UNITY ASSET STORE AND EXTERNAL TOOLS

In game development, time is often as valuable as skill. As a developer, you may find yourself needing resources such as art, sound, or even complex systems that would otherwise take weeks to create. Fortunately, Unity provides a convenient way to speed up this process through the **Unity Asset Store**. This chapter explores how you can leverage the Asset Store and other external tools to boost your productivity, create a more polished game, and streamline your development process. We'll also discuss the pros and cons of using free versus paid assets and how they can impact your game's final outcome.

Using Assets from Unity's Asset Store

1. Introduction to the Unity Asset Store The **Unity Asset Store** is an online marketplace where developers can buy and sell assets for their Unity projects. It's home to millions of assets that can save you time and effort by providing ready-made solutions for your game. These assets range from textures and 3D models to complex game systems like AI controllers, physics engines, and UI elements.

By purchasing or downloading free assets from the store, you can accelerate your development without needing to spend days or even weeks creating everything from scratch.

2. Types of Assets Available

- **Art Assets**: This includes 3D models, textures, sprites, animations, and UI elements. Whether you need stylized characters for a platformer or realistic models for an FPS, the Asset Store has you covered.
- **Sound and Music**: There are countless sound effects, background music tracks, and ambient sounds available. Many of these are categorized by game genre (e.g., fantasy, sci-fi, horror) to make it easier for you to find what you need.
- **Tools and Scripts**: A wide range of code and frameworks can help you speed up development. For example, you might find scripts for character movement, enemy AI, or even game management systems that handle things like scoring, progression, and save states.
- **Plugins and Editor Extensions**: Many tools are designed to enhance the Unity Editor itself. These can include tools for better workflow management, visual scripting, lighting systems, and more.

3. Integrating Assets from the Asset Store Once you find an asset that suits your needs, importing it into your Unity project is straightforward. You can either download assets directly through the Unity Editor or via the Asset Store website, and they'll be added to your project's **Assets** folder automatically.

While using assets from the store can significantly save time, you should still ensure that these assets integrate well with your game's art style and mechanics. Always check if the asset is customizable or if it fits your overall game's theme.

External Tools for Art, Sound, and Scripting

1. External Art Tools While Unity offers robust tools for creating 3D models and 2D sprites, many developers prefer to use specialized art programs for creating assets before importing them into Unity. Here are some popular tools:

- **Blender**: A free and open-source 3D modeling software that's incredibly powerful for creating models, animations, and textures. Blender's flexibility allows developers to create highly detailed and optimized assets for Unity.
- **Adobe Photoshop / GIMP**: For creating 2D sprites, textures, and UI elements, Photoshop is an industry-standard, though GIMP is a popular free alternative.

- **Aseprite**: This tool is widely used for pixel art, an essential art style for many indie developers.
- **Substance Painter**: A tool for creating realistic textures and materials that can be exported into Unity. Perfect for high-fidelity 3D models.

2. External Sound Tools Sound design plays a critical role in immersing players. While Unity supports basic audio features, you may want to use dedicated tools for creating or editing sounds:

- **Audacity**: A free, open-source audio editor that can help you record, edit, and clean up sound effects and voiceovers.
- **FL Studio / Ableton Live**: These are professional-level music production tools for creating game music and sound effects. Both have robust features for layering sounds, creating complex compositions, and editing audio.
- **Freesound.org**: An online repository of free sound effects that can be used for your game. It's a great resource for quickly gathering background sounds, UI clicks, and environmental noises.

3. External Scripting Tools Writing scripts in Unity is mostly done through the **C# programming language** within the built-in **MonoDevelop** or **Visual Studio** environments. However, there are additional tools that can speed up scripting and improve productivity:

- **Visual Studio Code**: A lightweight, customizable text editor that supports C# through plugins. It's faster than Visual Studio and provides a great environment for coding.
- **JetBrains Rider**: A powerful IDE designed for Unity development. Many developers prefer it over Visual Studio due to its faster performance and deeper integration with Unity.

Free vs Paid Assets and Their Impact on Game Development

1. Free Assets

- **Pros**: Free assets can be a great way to start development without a financial investment. Unity itself offers many free assets on the Asset Store, and other resources like **OpenGameArt.org** also provide free 2D and 3D assets.
  - **Lower Development Costs**: If you're on a budget, free assets can help you develop a prototype or even a complete game without spending money.

    - **Time-Saving**: With free assets, you can focus on core gameplay mechanics instead of spending time creating every little detail.

- **Cons**: While free assets are incredibly helpful, they might come with limitations. For example:
    - **Quality**: Some free assets might not be optimized for Unity, which could affect performance. The quality of art or code may also be inconsistent, and you may not find exactly what you need.
    - **Generic Look**: Free assets are available to everyone, which means your game could end up looking like others that use the same assets. This can hinder originality if you aren't careful about customization.

2. Paid Assets

- **Pros**: Paid assets tend to be of higher quality and offer more advanced features. The creators of paid assets usually put more effort into supporting and updating their products.
    - **Polished**: Paid assets often come with better documentation, optimized performance, and more complex functionality.
    - **Customizability**: Many paid assets allow for customization, and some come with additional

tools that can help streamline your development process.

- **Cons**: Of course, there are some trade-offs:
    - **Cost**: If you're working with a tight budget, purchasing multiple paid assets could become expensive, especially for larger projects.
    - **Over-Reliance**: Using too many paid assets can make your game feel too reliant on third-party tools. If the developer stops supporting the asset or updates it for newer versions of Unity, you may face compatibility issues.

3. When to Use Free vs Paid Assets

- **Early Development**: During prototyping or proof of concept, free assets are often more than sufficient. You can focus on testing gameplay mechanics without worrying too much about aesthetics.
- **Final Polishing**: Once your game is near completion and you want to add that extra layer of polish, it might be time to invest in high-quality paid assets. This is particularly important for art, sound, and custom scripts that need to match your vision.

Summary

Unity's Asset Store and external tools provide a wealth of resources to speed up your development process, whether you're building 2D or 3D games. By strategically using both free and paid assets, you can create a more polished product without reinventing the wheel. The key is to balance efficiency with creativity, using assets that help you focus on what matters most—your game's design and gameplay. Keep in mind the pros and cons of both free and paid assets, and always ensure that your game maintains a unique identity, even if you're borrowing resources from external sources.

CHAPTER 25

ADVANCED SCRIPTING AND OPTIMIZATION TECHNIQUES

As you progress in your game development journey with Unity, understanding the intricacies of **advanced scripting** and mastering **performance optimization** techniques are key to creating efficient, smooth-running games. This chapter dives deeper into Unity scripting, offering you powerful techniques and best practices for developing sophisticated, high-performing games. Additionally, we will explore **design patterns** commonly used in game development, such as **Singleton** and **Factory patterns**, and how they can enhance your coding architecture.

By the end of this chapter, you'll be equipped with the knowledge to improve your game's performance on both **mobile and desktop platforms**, as well as implement **elegant and reusable code** that scales well for larger projects.

Diving Deeper into Unity Scripting

Unity's scripting system is built on the **C# programming language**, and mastering it is essential for advanced game development. While the basics of scripting focus on moving objects or handling simple interactions, there's so much more you can achieve when you dive deeper into advanced topics. In this section, we'll cover some key areas where you can refine your scripting skills.

1. Understanding Unity's Lifecycle Methods The `MonoBehaviour` class offers several **event functions** that Unity automatically calls at various points during the game loop. Understanding when to use each of these functions is crucial for efficient game behavior.

- **Awake()**: Called when the script instance is being loaded. It's typically used for initialization before any Start() calls.
- **Start()**: Called before the first frame update. It's used for any setup that needs to happen just before the game starts.
- **Update()**: Called once per frame, ideal for constantly updating your game's mechanics (e.g., moving an object).
- **FixedUpdate()**: Called at a consistent rate, used for physics-based calculations.
- **LateUpdate()**: Called after all Update functions have been executed, often used for camera movement or following objects.

2. Advanced Scripting Concepts

- **Coroutines**: Coroutines allow you to run tasks over time, making it easier to perform actions like animations, timed events, or delays without freezing the main thread.

  Example:

```
csharp
CopyEdit
IEnumerator WaitForSecondsAndPrint()
{
    yield return new WaitForSeconds(2);
    Debug.Log("2 seconds have passed");
}
```

- **Events and Delegates**: These are used for managing callbacks and decoupling code. Instead of directly calling methods, you can define events and have other objects subscribe to them. This is especially useful in complex games where you want different systems to interact without tightly coupling them.

  Example:

```
csharp
CopyEdit
public event Action OnPlayerDeath;
```

- **Linq Queries**: In more advanced scripting, using **LINQ (Language Integrated Query)** can help you manipulate data collections such as arrays or lists in an efficient, readable way. For example:

```
csharp
CopyEdit
var highScores = scores.Where(score =>
score >= 100).OrderByDescending(score =>
score);
```

Advanced Performance Optimizations for Mobile and Desktop

One of the main challenges in game development is **optimizing performance** to ensure that your game runs smoothly, especially on lower-end devices or when targeting both mobile and desktop platforms. Optimization can involve both **CPU** and **GPU** performance, so it's essential to consider the following techniques:

1. Reducing Draw Calls Draw calls represent the number of times the GPU is asked to draw something to the screen. Reducing the number of draw calls can significantly improve performance, particularly on mobile devices.

- **Static Batching**: Combine static objects into larger meshes. Unity can group static objects together, reducing the number of draw calls.

- **Dynamic Batching**: For smaller objects, dynamic batching groups meshes together during runtime to reduce draw calls.
- **Using Sprite Atlases**: Combine multiple textures into a single image, so you can draw many sprites in one call. Unity provides **Sprite Atlases** to make this process easier.

2. Optimizing Physics Calculations Physics can quickly become expensive, especially with complex collisions or many moving objects. Here are some ways to reduce overhead:

- **Use simplified colliders** (e.g., BoxCollider2D or CircleCollider2D) instead of MeshColliders for static or dynamic objects.
- **Layer-based collision**: Set up layers for different objects and define collision rules only between relevant layers. This reduces unnecessary calculations.
- **Disable unnecessary physics**: Turn off physics calculations for objects that are not currently interacting with the player or other important game elements.

3. Memory Management Memory leaks and inefficient memory usage can significantly impact game performance. Below are a few practices to improve memory management:

- **Object Pooling**: Reuse objects instead of constantly creating and destroying them. This is especially important for objects that are frequently instantiated, like bullets or enemies.

- **Garbage Collection**: C# uses garbage collection, but frequent instantiation and destruction of objects can trigger unwanted pauses in the game. Minimize allocations during gameplay and consider reusing objects instead of creating new ones.

4. Mobile-Specific Optimizations When targeting mobile devices, performance is even more critical due to hardware limitations. Consider these tips:

- **Quality Settings**: Unity allows you to adjust the **Quality Settings** based on the platform. For mobile, reduce texture resolutions, disable certain post-processing effects, and use simpler shaders.
- **Frame Rate Limiting**: Limit the frame rate to something reasonable, like 30 FPS for mobile devices. This can save a lot of power and reduce heat generation on mobile devices.

Utilizing Design Patterns in Game Development

Design patterns are solutions to common problems that have been refined over time. In game development, certain patterns can help you organize your code, reduce duplication, and improve maintainability. Let's explore a couple of common patterns that are particularly useful in Unity game development.

1. Singleton Pattern The **Singleton** pattern ensures that a class has only one instance, which is accessible globally. This is useful for managing game states or other global systems that need to persist across scenes or gameplay sessions (e.g., GameManager, AudioManager).

Example:

```
csharp
CopyEdit
public class GameManager : MonoBehaviour
{
    public static GameManager Instance;

    void Awake()
    {
        if (Instance == null)
        {
            Instance = this;
            DontDestroyOnLoad(gameObject);
        }
        else
        {
            Destroy(gameObject);
        }
    }
```

}

2. Factory Pattern The **Factory** pattern allows you to create objects without specifying the exact class of the object to be created. This is especially useful when creating enemies, power-ups, or weapons that can be dynamically instantiated based on certain conditions.

Example:

```
csharp
CopyEdit
public class EnemyFactory : MonoBehaviour
{
    public    GameObject    CreateEnemy(EnemyType
type)
    {
        switch (type)
        {
            case EnemyType.Zombie:
                return
Instantiate(zombiePrefab);
            case EnemyType.Skeleton:
                return
Instantiate(skeletonPrefab);
            default:
                return null;
        }
    }
```

```
}
```

3. Observer Pattern The **Observer** pattern allows a system to notify other systems of changes without them needing to directly communicate. This is often used for event-driven programming, such as updating the UI when the player's health changes.

Example:

```
csharp
CopyEdit
public class HealthSystem : MonoBehaviour
{
    public event Action<int> OnHealthChanged;

    private int health;

    public void ChangeHealth(int amount)
    {
        health += amount;
        OnHealthChanged?.Invoke(health);
    }
}
```

Summary

Mastering advanced scripting in Unity and applying optimization techniques is key to building efficient and maintainable games. By understanding Unity's lifecycle methods, utilizing advanced features like coroutines and delegates, and adopting best practices such as **Object Pooling**, **Layered Collision**, and **Memory Management**, you can ensure smooth performance across both mobile and desktop platforms. Additionally, implementing design patterns such as **Singleton**, **Factory**, and **Observer** can help structure your game code in a way that is both reusable and scalable. With these techniques, you'll be well on your way to creating polished, high-performance games.

CHAPTER 26

TESTING YOUR GAME

In game development, testing is a critical phase that ensures the final product is polished, engaging, and free from bugs. No matter how good your game design or coding is, thorough testing is essential to guarantee a smooth experience for players. In this chapter, we'll explore the different types of testing that are vital to creating a successful game, including **playtesting**, **automated testing**, and **performance testing**. These processes will help you identify and fix issues early, ensuring your game works as intended on all devices.

Importance of Playtesting: Gathering Feedback

Playtesting is one of the most vital forms of testing. It involves having real players interact with your game and providing feedback based on their experiences. This form of testing helps you identify issues that might not be apparent during development, such as game difficulty, player engagement, and overall enjoyment. Here's how to approach it effectively:

1. Organizing Playtests

- **Early Playtesting**: Don't wait until the end of development to start playtesting. The earlier you test, the sooner you can identify fundamental design flaws. Start by testing small gameplay loops or even prototypes to gather early feedback.
- **Target Audience**: Choose testers who represent your target audience. If your game is meant for casual players, test it with people who are not experienced gamers. This will give you valuable insight into how intuitive and accessible the game is for newcomers.
- **Diverse Feedback**: Ensure you gather feedback from a variety of players with different skill levels and preferences. This will help you address problems related to difficulty, accessibility, and user interface.

2. Key Areas to Test During Playtesting

- **Gameplay Mechanics**: Are the controls intuitive? Does the player understand how to progress in the game? Are the objectives clear?
- **Game Balance**: Is the difficulty curve too steep? Are there any mechanics that are overpowered or underpowered? Playtesting can help you adjust these elements to create a more enjoyable experience.
- **Bug Detection**: Bugs and glitches can disrupt the flow of the game. Playtesters can often uncover bugs that were overlooked during development.

3. Gathering and Analyzing Feedback

- **Observations**: Watch how players interact with the game. Pay attention to where they get stuck, frustrated, or lose interest. This is often more revealing than verbal feedback.
- **Surveys and Interviews**: After playtesting sessions, conduct surveys or interviews to get direct feedback from players. Ask specific questions about the gameplay experience, level design, UI, and performance.
- **Iterate Based on Feedback**: Use the feedback to iterate on your game. It's not just about fixing bugs; it's about refining your design and making the game more enjoyable.

Automated Testing and Debugging

While playtesting is invaluable for identifying user-facing issues, **automated testing** can help detect underlying bugs and issues that would be time-consuming to catch manually. Automated testing is especially useful when working with large projects, as it can quickly verify that your code works as intended.

1. Types of Automated Tests

- **Unit Tests**: These tests focus on individual pieces of code (functions or methods) and ensure they work as expected.

For instance, you could write a unit test to verify that a player's health decreases correctly when taking damage.

Example:

```
csharp
CopyEdit
[Test]
public                                          void
TestPlayerHealthDecreasesOnDamage()
{
    Player player = new Player();
    player.TakeDamage(10);
    Assert.AreEqual(90, player.health);
}
```

- **Integration Tests**: These tests check if different parts of your game code work together as expected. For example, you might test the interaction between your player controller, enemy AI, and the game's health system.
- **UI Tests**: Ensure that all user interfaces respond properly. Automated UI testing can simulate interactions such as pressing buttons, navigating menus, and checking for correct UI updates.
- **Regression Tests**: As you add new features or fix bugs, regression testing helps ensure that changes haven't caused new problems or broken existing functionality.

2. Debugging in Unity Unity provides powerful debugging tools that can help you identify issues during development. Use **breakpoints**, **log statements**, and the **Console window** to track variables and states in real-time.

- **Log Statements**: The `Debug.Log` function is commonly used to output values to the console during runtime. You can use it to track the flow of execution and identify where things go wrong.

  ```
  csharp
  CopyEdit
  Debug.Log("Player Health: " +
  player.health);
  ```

- **Breakpoints**: Set breakpoints in Visual Studio or your preferred IDE to pause the game at a specific line of code. This allows you to step through your code line by line and inspect variable values.
- **Profiler**: Unity's **Profiler** window allows you to track performance in real time. Use it to identify bottlenecks or areas where your game is consuming too many resources.

Performance Testing Across Devices

Performance testing ensures that your game runs smoothly across all target platforms, whether it's PC, mobile, or console. This testing helps identify issues related to **frame rates**, **load times**, and **resource usage**, which are particularly important for mobile devices that have more limited processing power.

1. Mobile-Specific Performance Testing

- **Frame Rate**: Test the frame rate on a variety of devices. Aim for 30-60 frames per second (FPS) on most devices, as anything lower can lead to a poor user experience.
- **Memory Usage**: Monitor how much memory your game uses and ensure it fits within the limits of target devices. Unity's **Profiler** tool is essential for analyzing memory consumption and garbage collection.
- **Battery Usage**: On mobile devices, battery life is a concern. Test how long your game runs on a full charge and optimize it to reduce power consumption.

2. Stress Testing and Load Testing

- **Stress Testing**: Simulate high-stress conditions by adding many objects to the scene or running complex scripts. This helps you identify performance drops and areas that need optimization.
- **Load Testing**: Test your game's performance during heavy loads, such as when the player is near a large number of enemies or objects. Ensure that performance remains consistent even under intense conditions.

3. Cross-Platform Testing If you're targeting multiple platforms (PC, mobile, consoles), it's essential to test the game on each device. Performance can vary significantly between platforms, so ensure you're optimizing for the lowest common denominator.

- **Unity's Build Settings**: Use Unity's **Build Settings** to export and test your game on different platforms. Optimize settings for each platform, such as graphics quality, resolution, and input methods.
- **Touch Input Testing (Mobile)**: If you're building for mobile, ensure that touch controls are responsive and consistent. Test your game on various screen sizes and resolutions to ensure a smooth experience on all devices.

Summary

Testing is an essential step in game development that ensures your game is fun, functional, and performant across all devices. **Playtesting** provides valuable feedback from real players, helping you refine gameplay and design. **Automated testing** allows you to catch bugs early and efficiently check for issues in your code. Finally, **performance testing** ensures your game runs smoothly on all target devices, whether on mobile or desktop. By integrating these testing techniques into your development workflow, you can create a polished, high-quality game that players will love.

CHAPTER 27

GAME DEVELOPMENT TRENDS AND NEXT STEPS

By the time you reach this point, you've gone from setting up Unity for the first time to building a complete, functional 2D game. That's a solid foundation. But game development isn't something you ever really "finish" learning. Tools evolve, player expectations shift, and new platforms and workflows show up all the time. This chapter is about what's happening *now* in 2D game development, what other tools are out there besides Unity, and where you can go from here—whether you want to work in a studio, go indie, or just keep leveling up.

Current Trends in 2D Game Development

Let's not pretend 2D games are a thing of the past. Despite all the buzz around AAA 3D titles and photorealistic graphics, 2D games continue to hold their own in the market—especially among indie developers. But like everything in tech, the landscape keeps shifting.

1. Retro but Modern Pixel art is still popular, but people expect polish. Games like *Celeste* and *Dead Cells* show how high-resolution effects, dynamic lighting, and fluid animations can coexist with a retro aesthetic.

2. Procedural Generation Randomly generated levels aren't new, but now they're better—smarter layouts, more variety, and just enough unpredictability to keep things interesting. Players want replayability without repetition.

3. Narrative-Driven 2D Games Storytelling is becoming a bigger deal in 2D. Text-based games, visual novels, and dialogue-heavy platformers are trending, especially when paired with solid writing and voice acting.

4. Accessibility Features There's increasing demand for games that everyone can play. That means customizable controls, colorblind modes, assist options, and more thought given to UI and UX. Unity makes it relatively easy to implement these, but not enough devs do it.

5. Cross-Platform Development Players switch between platforms more than ever, so devs are expected to launch on PC, mobile, and sometimes even console. That's pushing tools like Unity to keep improving their build pipelines.

6. Minimalist Game Design A growing number of developers are leaning into simplicity—minimal art styles, simple mechanics, tight controls. Think *Limbo* or *Thomas Was Alone*. It's about precision over flash.

Looking Beyond Unity: Other Tools and Frameworks

Unity is great for a lot of reasons, but it's not the only option. Depending on your goals and the scope of your future projects, you might want to explore alternatives—either because they're lighter, more open, or better suited for a specific genre.

1. Godot Engine

- Free and open-source
- Smaller install size, lightweight projects
- Scene-based structure similar to Unity, but simpler in some ways
- Uses GDScript (Python-like), with growing support for C#

2. GameMaker Studio 2

- Very popular for 2D games
- Streamlined workflow for rapid prototyping
- Drag-and-drop interface for beginners, plus a scripting language (GML)
- Great for mobile and desktop games

3. Cocos2d-x

- Open-source and C++ based, with Lua and JavaScript options
- Widely used in mobile development, especially in Asia
- Not beginner-friendly, but very performant

4. Phaser (HTML5)

- JavaScript-based, browser-friendly
- Great for quick prototypes, web games, and mobile-friendly HTML5 experiences
- Lightweight and open-source

5. Unreal Engine

- Overkill for most 2D games, but still possible
- If you ever decide to move into 3D development or visual-heavy games, knowing both Unity and Unreal is a plus

Unity still offers the best mix of power, community support, and platform reach, but it's not a bad idea to be aware of what else is out there—especially if licensing, platform constraints, or personal preferences push you in a different direction.

Continuing Your Growth as a Game Developer

You've learned the tools, built a game, and (hopefully) released it or shared it with testers. Now what?

1. Join the Community

- Follow Unity forums, Reddit subs like r/gamedev and r/IndieDev, and Discord servers. You'll learn a lot by helping others troubleshoot their issues and seeing how other devs approach problems.
- Participate in game jams like **Ludum Dare**, **GMTK Jam**, or **Global Game Jam**. They're great for practice, networking, and building a portfolio under pressure.

2. Build a Portfolio

- Keep making games. Even small ones. Especially small ones.
- Publish your projects on Itch.io or Steam. It shows initiative, and the feedback will be invaluable.
- Don't just show your games—talk about them. What worked? What didn't? What did you learn?

3. Learn the Business Side

- If you're thinking of going indie, you'll need to know more than just Unity. Marketing, user acquisition, monetization models, and publishing platforms are worth understanding.
- Read postmortems. Lots of them. Developers often write brutally honest breakdowns of their failures and

successes—and you'll learn more from those than any tutorial.

4. Keep Learning

- Tools change. Best practices change. Trends come and go.
- Stay current with Unity updates, engine changes, and new asset packages.
- Consider branching into related areas—UI/UX design, sound design, procedural generation, shader programming. Being T-shaped (broad skills with depth in one area) makes you a lot more adaptable.

Final Thoughts

You've got the foundation now—Unity setup, scripting, UI, polish, release, and beyond. You understand not just how to build a game, but how to *finish* one. That's a skill most people never reach. Whether you want to keep refining this project, start a new one, or build a career in game development, you've got what you need to move forward.

The next game you make? That's where everything really starts to click.

www.ingramcontent.com/pod-product-compliance
Lightning Source LLC
LaVergne TN
LVHW051320050326
832903LV00031B/3275